A HISTORY OF GRAVESEND

James Benson,

A History of
GRAVESEND

OR

A HISTORICAL PERAMBULATION
OF
GRAVESEND AND NORTHFLEET

by

JAMES BENSON

Revised and Edited
by

ROBERT HEATH HISCOCK,
LL.B., F.S.A.

PHILLIMORE

First published 1976, reprinted 1981

PHILLIMORE & CO. LTD.,
London and Chichester

Head Office: Shopwyke Hall,
Chichester, Sussex, England

ISBN 0 85033 242 7

Printed and bound in Great Britain by
PLYMOUTH WEB OFFSET LTD.
Plymouth, Devon

CONTENTS

Part One

LIST OF PLATES

ACKNOWLEDGMENTS

Frontispiece: Gravesend and Dartford Reporter Limited; Plates 1, 3, 4, 5, 6, 7, 8, 11, 13, 14, 15, 16: Gravesham Public Library, Gould Collection; Plate 2: Gravesham Public Library; Plate 9: J. Benson; Plates 10, 12: J. S. Kean.

LIST OF FIGURES

PREFACE

The manuscript on which this perambulation is based was first typed by Mr. Benson in 1954. It then comprised the section relating to Gravesend, although a section on Northfleet, together with two or three appendices were planned. He was not altogether satisfied with it and put it aside to revise and complete, but other projects intervened, It was only after the death of his wife early in 1972 that at my suggestion he started work on it again, intending to give it to the Gravesend Historical Society for possible publication. At the time of his death on 4 June 1972 he had only revised a few sections.

The principle on which this history has been compiled has necessitated a thorough revision of all the sections to bring it up to date, due to the extensive demolitions and rebuilding which has taken place in the town during the last 20 years. In addition I have added a section on Northfleet, making use in part of the material which Mr. Benson collected for his series of articles in the *Gravesend Reporter* on 'Northfleet through the Ages', and Mr. A. F. Allen has added an Appendix on the piers.

On 1 April 1974 both Gravesend and Northfleet became part of the new Gravesham Borough Council. The name 'Gravesham' appears only in the Domesday Book 1086, and was probably an error of the Norman scribe. It was 'Gravesend' in the Domesday *Monarchorum c.* 1100, and 'Gravesende' in the *Textus Roffensis c.* 1100. It is strange that this 'clerical error', has now been adopted for the name of the new Council.

Mr. Benson, who was born on 12 December 1878, had lived all his life in Northfleet and Gravesend, and had a quite remarkable memory not only of events, but also for dates. His articles in the *Gravesend Reporter* on local history over the last 25 years did much to stimulate interest in the history of the locality and his researches into local archives and documents increased considerably our knowledge of the district. On his 90th birthday the Historical Society presented him with an illuminated address, the work of the late Mr. J. S. Kean, which is now in the local museum. It is hoped that the publication of this History may be some memorial to Mr. Benson and the work he did for local history in this area.

The photographic illustrations other than the picture of Mr. Benson are from the Gould Collection at the Gravesham public library and the line drawings are from various blocks in possession of the Gravesend Historical Society and the public library, including some given to the Society by Mr. A. J. Kean. The picture of Mr. Benson is from the *Gravesend and Dartford Reporter.*

My grateful thanks are due to Mr. Woods, A.L.A., and his staff at the Gravesend library, including Mr. P. Willis, to members of the Gravesend Historical Society, especially Miss A. T. B. Knowles, Messrs. A. G. Ridgers, V. T. C. Smith, E. R. Green, E. W. Tilley, E. C. Gunkel, and Mrs. Darby and her husband, who produced the plan; also to Mrs. S. Mackley for typing the manuscript. Its publication has been possible due to a most generous bequest to the Society under Mr. Benson's Will.

ROBERT H. HISCOCK

1976 *Chairman, Gravesend Historical Society*

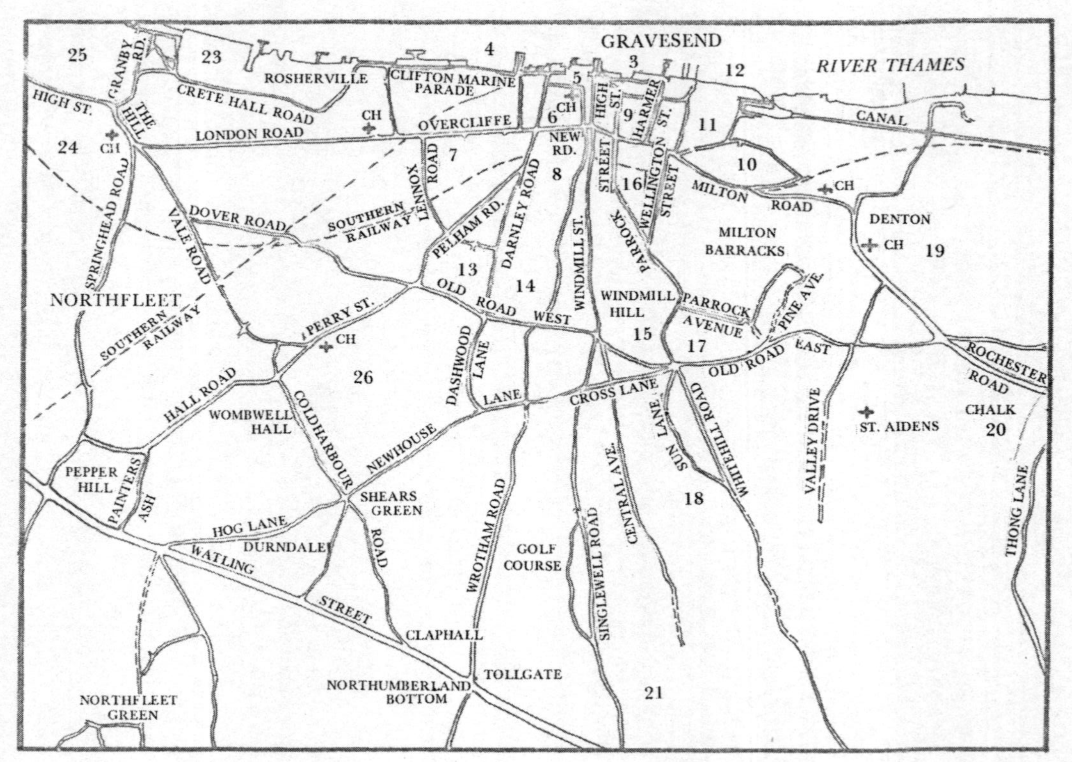
GRAVESEND
RIVER THAMES
CANAL
25
23
4
3
12
GRANBY RD.
ROSHERVILLE
CLIFTON MARINE PARADE
5
HIGH ST.
HARMER ST.
9
11
HIGH ST.
CRETE HALL ROAD
THE HILL
CH
OVERCLIFFE
6
CH
LONDON ROAD
24
CH
NEW RD.
STREET
WELLINGTON STREET
10
7
LENNOX ROAD
8
16
MILTON ROAD
CH
SPRINGHEAD ROAD
VALE ROAD
DOVER ROAD
SOUTHERN RAILWAY
PELHAM RD.
DARNLEY ROAD
WINDMILL ST.
PARROCK
MILTON BARRACKS
DENTON
CH
19
13
14
NORTHFLEET
OLD ROAD WEST
WINDMILL HILL
PARROCK AVENUE
PINE AVE.
SOUTHERN RAILWAY
PERRY ST.
CH
15
17
DASHWOOD LANE
OLD ROAD EAST
ROCHESTER ROAD
26
CROSS LANE
LANE
HALL ROAD
WOMBWELL HALL
COLDHARBOUR
SUN LANE
WHITEHILL ROAD
VALLEY DRIVE
ST. AIDENS
CHALK
20
NEWHOUSE
PEPPER HILL
PAINTERS ASH
SHEARS GREEN
CENTRAL AVE.
18
THONG LANE
HOG LANE
DURNDALE
ROAD
WROTHAM ROAD
SINGLEWELL ROAD
GOLF COURSE
WATLING STREET
CLAPHALL
TOLLGATE
NORTHUMBERLAND BOTTOM
21
NORTHFLEET GREEN

PART ONE

Chapter One

SURVEYING THE GROUND

THOSE UNFAMILIAR with the town of Gravesend, its situation and the contour of the district may not readily appreciate the reason for the choice of the summit of Windmill Hill as the starting-point of this perambulation of the town. The Hill has little discoverable history earlier than the 16th century, and that very meagre, but its height above the surrounding country provides a vantage-ground from which to view the district as a whole before visiting at closer quarters the buildings and streets possessing historical associations. When this survey was first contemplated around 1952 the view to the north from the Hill presented a homogenity which the last 20 years have destroyed. Then, most of the roofs were grey slate covering houses built between 1830 and 1860 in a fairly regular pattern of through roads with houses of three or four storeys, and smaller streets and houses in between. The clearance of the area between Windmill Street and Parrock Street and the erection of large blocks of flats with the multi-storey car park and municipal buildings, has completely altered the view, and the enormous chimneys of the power stations and cement works have provided a new dominant feature in the landscape.

Looking northwards one is conscious of the important part played by the River Thames in England's history. With the closure of the London docks the traffic on the river has diminished, but the presence of shipping in Gravesend Reach still provides a reminder of the link which has so long existed between the Thames and the continent of Europe as well as the remotest seaports of the world. There can have been few grander maritime sights than to witness from the summit of the hill in the mid-years of the 19th century the stately towers of square sail of the numerous clippers making their way up the river with cargoes of tea or grain, or wood, or spice, after having been blown across the oceans of the world.

The flat Essex shore, rising a mile or so back to a ridge upon which modern dwellings and blocks of flats have been built, provides a background for the scene: slightly more to the left, liners in Tilbury docks (opened in 1886 and since enlarged) being loaded or unloaded, or raised high in dry dock for overhaul, remind us of the many processes entailed in a maritime nation's economy. The building of the container terminal is further evidence of changing maritime methods.

On the Essex shore can be seen 'The World's End' with what was formerly the causeway for the cross ferry in front and to the right Tilbury Fort with its Carolean Water Gate build in 1682. The first defences here were provided during the reign of Henry VIII when a blockhouse was erected by the side of the river. The present bastioned fort (which is in the care of the Department of the Environment) was built between 1670 and 1683, according to a design of Sir Bernard de Gomme. To the east stands the Tilbury power station, built in the 1950s, and since considerably extended.

It will not be amiss at such a point in our thoughts to conjecture why Gravesend came to be the outer port of the firmly-established city of London. Was it not that in very early days when the river, unembanked, spread at high tide over the marshes east and west of Gravesend, the chalk spur reaching out to the tideway itself provided the first hard landing-ground upon which incoming sailor-men could find firm foothold. In addition to this, the landing place was exactly a tide away from London, so that whether the wind were fair or foul quick passage and safe anchorage were available, with shelter under the lee of the Kent and Essex shores. The hythe which existed at the foot of the present High Street in the 11th century was even at that date a landing-place with a few centuries' history behind it. Travellers to the new world in Tudor and later times frequently spent their last night in England at Gravesend at one of the local inns, such as the *Christopher*. The great East India company, founded in the 16th century, provisioned their ships at Gravesend, and had their own camp for their soldiers and sailors and their own hospitals here.

If one turns towards the south, one sees to-day a large built-up area spreading into the countryside, where 60 years ago one looked upon wheatfields, orchards and arable lands devoted to market garden produce. Until the last quarter of the 19th century Windmill Hill lay to the south of the town, and Singlewell and Chalk were isolated villages.

The Hill rises to about 169 feet above high tide level and consists of an outlier or capping of Thanet Sands in the middle of surrounding chalk a hundred or so feet deep. It owes its present name to the windmills built upon its summit at various times from the 16th century onwards. It was previously known as Ruggen, Rogge, Rounden, or Rouge Hill. Until the end of the 18th century it was rough, untilled ground, and the earlier name may have been a spelling of 'rough'. Beacons giving warning of the approach of invading forces were erected on the Hill in 1377 and again in 1588, and one was standing there in readiness for use in 1719, according to Dr. Harris's *History of Kent*.

Whether the Hill was used in Roman or Saxon times as a look-out is unknown. No evidence in the shape of pottery, coins or domestic articles have ever been found. The important Roman town of Vagniacae was some two miles away to the south-west at Springhead.

In the early 19th century Windmill Hill became the playground of London residents, who spent summer holidays in Gravesend or made day trips by steamers, engaging in donkey-rides and the fun-fair activities of the period, mounting the old mill erected in 1764, but by then only used as a means whereby a better view might be had of still farther horizons. A gallery at the height of 20 feet above the ground provided a look-out for visitors. Refreshment houses, the *Tivoli*, the *Belle Vue* on top of the Hill, the *Miller's Cottage* in Shrubbery Road, and other licensed houses carried on a thriving trade. With the decay of Gravesend as a holiday resort, the mill became derelict and was finally pulled down in 1894. The last remnant of the town's heyday, the *Belle Vue*, was destroyed by fire during the boisterous celebrations of Mafeking Night in 1900, the firemen's hoses being cut when they attempted to save it. The *Tivoli* hotel, to be noted when reaching Windmill Street, became an academy for Jewish youths and a synagogue in 1856, and remained in this use until the outbreak of war in 1914, when the school was removed elsewhere. Later, it has been employed as a social club and as an auctioneer's saleroom, and as a bingo club.

The Hill was purchased in 1843 by the Corporation, and in 1889 the lower slopes were acquired also. This enabled the foot of the Hill to be terraced and turned into pleasure and sports grounds. They were opened by the Lord Mayor of London in May 1902. The War Memorial was dedicated on 11 June 1922 and unveiled by Gen. Lord Horne. This was damaged by enemy aircraft during the 1939-45 war, and re-erected afterwards, when the names of those who perished in that war were added. Here a service of remembrance is held each year on the Sunday nearest to 11 November. The small granite stones on the Hill mark the site of the first bombs dropped on the town from a German zeppelin in June 1915.

As we turn west from the Windmill Gardens we shall pass the Veterans Club, erected and opened in 1954 as a social meeting-place and games centre for men above 60 years of age. It occupies the site of the Maze. The thoroughfare in which it is situated, Clarence Place, was known earlier as Lacey Terrace, from the name of the builder of many of its houses, Edward Lacey, who was mayor of Gravesend in 1850.

In this thoroughfare there was erected in 1873 Milton Congregational church (architect John Sulmar of London. It was intended to have a south-west tower). It was the outcome of a split in Princes Street Congregational church (see Chapter Four). It maintained a separate and useful ministry until 1955, and after closing, was used as a warehouse. In 1968 it became a Sikh temple for the local Indian community, who had previously had a temple at 55 Edwin Street.

Chapter Two

WINDMILL STREET AND HIGH STREET

WINDMILL STREET is the dividing line (with Singlewell Road, its continuation southwards, and High Street northwards) between the ancient parishes of Gravesend and Milton which (with the additions of Denton and Chalk and parts of Ifield, Cobham and Northfleet in 1935) made up the municipal borough of Gravesend as it existed until 1974. The majority of the houses in this street to the north of Clarence Place date back to the 1830s and 1840s. On the west side, where Wingfield Road is, was the site of a vast market garden in the 19th century known as Clark's, extending 200 yards north and south, and here was grown the Gravesend asparagus which was greatly sought after by West End gourmets in the late 18th century. As we turn right we see two large semi-detached houses on the west side, 'North House' and 'South House' (which were formerly one house) and until recently had iron fencing, the gate standards of which were decorated with the town arms. These were originally part of the railings in front of the town pier (see Chapter Three). Next to them is Sheppy Place, which formerly led to Baynard Castle, a castellated Gothic house, built in the early 19th century by Edward Lacey, a former mayor, used later as a girls' school, and demolished in 1953.

On the northern corner of Clarence Row was at one time the high-class boarding school known as Clarence House or Gutteridge's, where many lads of the district and beyond received an education for business and academic careers. Before becoming a school it was the *Clarence* hotel, giving its name to the houses in Clarence Row.

A wine and spirit retail store on the corner of South Street on the right demands attention as a former place of leisure and entertainment built in 1835 as Tulley's Bazaar. Here holidaymakers were welcome at all times of the day to listen to orchestral music free of charge, and purchase, if so inclined, mementos of their visit, or presents for friends. Round the sides were illuminated views of Italy and Switzerland, seen as through a porthole: refreshment could be obtained in the form of coffee and chocolate. In the evenings, concerts were given at prices ranging from about a shilling per person. Later, the building became the drill hall of the local Artillery Volunteers, with small cannon standing outside, and in 1890 a grocery and provision store known as Milton Hall Stores.

A few yards lower down is the Baptist church, erected in 1843, and nearly opposite was the Gravesend fire station and police headquarters of the town, erected in 1940 and demolished in 1973 and at present rebuilding. Immediately to the south of this is the Kent County Council divisional offices, erected in 1965. To the north lies the new Civic Centre and Woodville Halls, opened by the Duchess of Kent in 1968. The architect was H. T. Cadbury Brown. The site was formerly occupied by private houses on one of which was the date 1837, and a little further up a date of 1849. In 1924 a creche for mothers and young children was erected on the back garden of one of the houses, and was the forerunner of the present child clinics.

The new police station was opened on 30 June 1975 by Sir John Hill, H.M. Chief Inspector of Constabulary. Architect: D. F. Clayton, County Architect.

A very pleasantly laid-out public garden on the left on a 'flat-iron' site, known as Woodville Gardens, was formerly a burial ground of the town, and a few of the old tombstones are still to be seen against the north wall. This piece of ground was acquired in 1788 by the churchwardens of Gravesend to supplement the old graveyard of St. George's church. When the burial ground was first used it stood on the outskirts of the town. In the open space where now Windmill Street and Wrotham Road are joined, there once stood the 'pound', and in 1864 was the site for the election hustings.

The open space known as Railway Place was before the coming of the South Eastern Railway in 1849 occupied by wooden cottages and here, too, the donkeys which provided rides on Windmill Hill and the goat-drawn chaises for children were stabled. Manor Road, on the east side of the street, is stated to have been so called from the existence there of an office where manorial quit-rents were paid, but the evidence for this is very meagre. Pocock informs us that the Court Baron for the Manor of Gravesend was opened (and then adjourned) in a piece of ground called the Pound Field, which was opposite the end of Manor Road. This field and Manor Road were both in the parish of Milton, although apparently part of the Manor of Gravesend. On a map of the early 19th century Manor Road is marked as 'The Land Way', the ground at its eastern end being then all open fields.

At the turn of the century many of the shops on the east side of Windmill Street were private houses with gardens in front, and except for a cobbler's adjoining the bridge there were no shops to the south of the railway until about 1925. Those on the western side have a longer history, and it is interesting to note that in the 18th century the street was known as Upper High Street.

Just before reaching the crossroad the public library deserves attention. Built of Ancaster stone and red brick, it was opened on 28 September 1905 by the mayor, G. M. Arnold. The cost of the building was obtained from a grant by the Scottish-American millionaire, Andrew Carnegie. The site was donated by subscriptions of £50 each from a number of local residents. The architect was Mr. E. J Bennett. In addition to its ordinary function of lending books and providing newspapers in the public reading room, its reference library possesses a wealth of reference books and material on local history.

Here and around the corner into King Street there stood until 1896 St. Thomas's almshouses, the successors of other gift houses bequeathed in 1624 by Henry Pinnock, Portreve of Gravesend in 1597, 1607 and 1613, for the benefit of the poor of Gravesend and Milton.

The almshouses which the present buildings superseded were built in 1834 of red brick with stone facings set on a plateau walled with brick and with a stretch of grass before. They replaced a group of weatherboard almshouses which appear in the earliest prints of King Street. When the Trustees disposed of the site the proceeds were used to build the present almshouses at the junction of Old Road and Upper Wrotham Road (see Chapter Twenty-five).

Hereabouts, where the streets cross, there was in earlier centuries what were known as St. Thomas's Waterings, where pilgrims to the shrine of St. Thomas à Becket stopped for rest and refreshment. This has caused the name of St. Thomas to be given to the almshouses. King Street, the road on the right, was known as late as the 18th century as St. Thomas's Street. In the 16th century it was known as Holy Water Street, as a house here, known as 'Holy Water', belonged to William Sidley or Sedley, who sold it to Henry Pinnock in 1624. Until 1801, when New Road was cut to provide a direct road to Northfleet, there was no break in the line of shops and houses on the western side from what is now Windmill Street to High Street.

The earliest mention of High Street, which we now enter, is of the year 1334, when property with houses thereon was conveyed to John Page the younger and Helen his wife, of Gravesend. This was in the parish of Milton, and was stated to be 'abutting upon High Street towards the west'. The High Street of that time was not a continuous line of houses as we see it to-day. Between what is now the site of the old Town Hall and the river there appears, according to a document of 1456, to have been only two houses on the Milton side of the street, until the riverside was reached, with one or two tenements on the Town Quay. It is probable that a channel ran down the middle of the street and that down its course went the unwanted domestic rubbish, washed by rains or periodical swillings with well water. The town's Second Charter of Incorporation, dated 1568 required every inhabitant 'to weekly cleanse before his door for the avoidance of evil odours' under a penalty of three shillings and fourpence.

Between the *Kent* public house and the junction with Royal Pier Road was a parcel of land belonging to the Abbot of the monastery of St. Mary Le Graces, Tower Hill, London. This was also part of the old manor of Parrock. The piece between the *Kent* and Bank Street was in the early part of the 15th century the site of Dame Anne's Hall. The other piece between Bank Street and Joe Coral's, turf accountants, was called Beelings or Baldwins Acre, and the rest of the land on the north was called Stonehawe or Stonehall.

William Bourne (*c.* 1565–1581), innkeeper, mathematician, gunner, and mercer, well-known for his writings on ordnance, inventions and navigation, owned messuages, tenements and gardens on the east side of the High Street.

By the late 18th century the street must have begun to assume something of the appearance it still had in the late 19th century, as Pocock, Gravesend's first historian (to whom reference will be made later), writes: 'almost every tradesman had a sign and in the night when the wind blew strong, a concert of squeaking music filled your ears with sounds not the most pleasant'. The demolition in 1928 of the *New Prince of Orange*, which occupied the site of Burton's, the tailors, and of Bryant and Rackstraws, at one time the leading drapery and haberdashery store in the town, on the opposite corner (now Woolworths), in 1957, has completely altered the appearance of this corner. High Street has doubled in width. It was previously eight feet wide.

In 1963 the shoe shop at 43 High Street was demolished, and Mr. E. W. Tilley of the Gravesend Historical Society excavated the site from which it was apparent that a shoe shop had existed on the site for 150 years. From the contents of various rubbish pits, however, there was evidence that the site had been occupied continuously since the 13th century with slight slackening off in the 14th and 15th centuries, with extensive occupation beginning again in the 17th century.

Robert Pocock (1760–1830) was born and lived in High Street for very many years, and on the front of the house on the west side, where he carried on his trade of printer, and from which his *History of Gravesend and Milton* was published in 1797, a blue-enamelled iron tablet was affixed in 1888 by G. M. Arnold, mayor of Gravesend 1896–7 and 1904–6. This records the fact that it was here that Pocock set up the first printing press in the town in 1786. Here, too, in Pocock's youth, John Wesley visited his friend the Rev. John Dolman, vicar of Chalk, who had apartments with Mrs. Pocock

(Pocock's mother), spending the night here with .his friend.

Robert Pocock was a man of wide interests, one of which was botany: he also badgered sailors to bring him natural history specimens from foreign lands. Ill-fortune overtook him towards the end of his life, his property being sold to defray his debts: later historians owe a great deal to his enthusiasm for recording historical events.

Passing Jury Street, the narrow opening on the left, it may be observed that until this was cut in 1846-7 there was no outlet from High Street other than pedestrian footways. A fire which occurred in the earlier year, and which destroyed much property in the street, provided the opportunity to cut through into Princes Street, and the name of the street commemorates the fact that a jury sat to assess the amount of the damage and the cost of the change made.

To the north of Jury Street was *The Catherine Wheel*, which bore on its front the year of its erection, 1686. Half of this building still remains and is now 56 High Street.

The old Town Hall stands in the parish of Milton, with the market at its rear. It was erected in 1764, C. Sloane, who designed St. George's church, being its architect. In 1836 the old front was removed and the present one substituted by Amon Henry Wilds. Three large figures adorned the pediment until 1939 when they were removed, being thought unsafe: these represented Minerva, Truth and Justice. This building was used as the Town Hall until 1968 when the present Civic Centre was opened. It now houses only the Magistrates Courts. The old Council Chamber is now used as the No. 1 Court. It still contains the portraits of former members of the council and town clerks. Until 1940 the police station was underneath on the north side. These rooms now house the local museum and collections belonging to the library and the Gravesend Historical Society.

Gravesend's first Town Hall was built in 1573, five years after the Borough received its second Charter of Incorporation. The First Charter was granted by Queen Elizabeth in 1562 and the second (which required one Portreve instead of two) in 1568. This Charter required that the Portreve,

1.–*The Catherine Wheel, c.* 1840

Jurats and Inhabitants meet in some convenient place to transact municipal business. The lease of the ground upon which the Town Hall now stands was then held on a 2,000-year lease of the Manor of Parrock by William Child of Northfleet: the new Corporation acquired an under-lease, and the Town Hall was built.

The Common Market which the Charter required the Corporation to hold once a week was established between the new building and what is now known as Queen Street. At first an open space, it was later converted into two covered ways with stone columns supporting the roof, but with an uncovered centre area. This remained until the present market hall was built in 1897, when the columns were removed to the grounds of Milton Hall (see Chapter Seventeen, p. 110).

Before the new frontage was added to the Town Hall in 1836, and indeed from the first Town Hall's erection, space was provided for a 'cage' for the incarceration of prisoners, and stocks were here set up. The parish of Milton, in which the cage stood, had to provide fresh straw for it periodically, and keep it clean. This cage was on the north side of the Town Hall.

This place in our guide seems the most suitable to mention the arms of the town which, on the obtaining of the Second Charter, was a device of a boat with one mast, its sail furled, rowed by five hooded rowers and steered by a porcupine. (A replica in metal can be seen on the south gate of Milton church.) The porcupine is held to be a compliment to Sir Henry Sydney, Steward of the Honour of Otford, in whose stewardship Gravesend and Milton were, and whose arms embodied a porcupine: the rowers denoted Gravesend's association with the waterside. When the town was granted its Third Charter in 1632, the Duke of Lennox was prominent in securing the charter, and the city fathers substituted the Duke's arms for the earlier one, viz.: a castle with a bull's head in its centre, and the Latin words 'Decus et Tutamen', which are held to mean 'My Glory and Strength'.

Lower down the street on the east side is Bank Street, cut through in 1850 following another extensive fire, and so named from the bank that stood on its southern corner. The first branch of a joint stock bank was opened in Gravesend in 1837 at 17 High Street by the Surrey, Kent and Sussex Banking Company, later the London and County, and now the National Westminster. After the fire of 1850 the bank was rebuilt at 16 High Street. In 1864 they moved to new premises at 24 High Street, next to the old Town Hall and formerly the *Freemason's Arms,* and in 1901 the present branch in King Street was opened. The architect was Mr. A. Williams, Messrs. Creaton and Co. were the builders, the work commencing in 1898 on the site of the old almshouses. Barclays Bank followed the London and County at 24 High Street, moving to King Street about 1930.

In the early 17th century the *Ship* inn stood just below the present Bank Street where, on his second visit to England in 1614, King Christian of Denmark dined with his nephew, the short-lived Prince Henry, son of James I, when they were passing through Gravesend to review the fleet in Chatham Dockyard.

Farther down on the right there stood until the early years of the 20th century the *Bull* hotel (No. 6), itself a successor of a licensed house where lived Henry Pinnock, whose will provided the almshouses mentioned above. In his will he speaks of 'My mansion house called the Bull in Milton' and leaving it to Thomas Lord requires that he should 'pay to our Sovereign Lord the King £3 every year for the wine licence out of the rent'. The *Bull* is also mentioned in a conveyance of 1464.

Before leaving High Street, reference must be made of the Great Fire of 1727 which consumed the whole of the lower part of the street, much of West Street, and part of East Street opposite. It had its origin in a farm building just south of St. George's churchyard, near to Princes Street, where Wakefield Street now stands. On the early morning of 24 August of that year a doctor named Mann, who resided in High Street nearly opposite the Town Hall, was returning from a call and noticed a small fire which he said 'could have been covered by a hat'. He stabled his horse and when he returned the fire, fanned by a strong south-west wind, was beyond control. Inhabitants, roused from sleep, fought the flames aided by soldiery, but it gained so rapidly that not only the streets mentioned above suffered destruction, but also the parish church. Dwelling-houses and shops to the number of 120 were laid in ruins, and the loss in money value was variously set between £120,000 and £200,000.

When rebuilding was carried out the shops and houses in the streets were again rebuilt mainly of timber and some of these fell a ready prey to other conflagrations in 1731, 1748, 1799, 1845, 1850 and 1857. There are still a small group of houses on the east side of the street, Nos 77–83, which are the last of those built in the 1730s after the fire of 1727.

A scheme for widening West Street and East Street recently carried out has necessitated the demolition among others of the corner shop, whose predecessor on the site was bequeathed by David Varchell in 1703 to provide the annual gift of money and bread to the poor which used to be distributed in St. George's church on the Sunday before Christmas, when the rector preached a charity sermon.

2.–High Street from the Pier, *c.* 1840

Chapter Three

THE TOWN PIER

IN MOST TOWNS there is an area where history is more closely packed than anywhere else, and Gravesend is no exception. Most often it is the market-place that can claim this distinction, but it is around the Town Pier square in this waterside town that the events of the centuries are most clearly seen. If it were possible to bring upon this square as upon a stage, with their attendant circumstances, all the important historical characters known to have embarked at this spot, what a varied and colourful assemblage it would be!

How many of the 'noble lordes, Knyghtes, squyers and oother about the noombre of cccc (400)' who accompanied the Count de la Roche in 1467 when he came from Burgundy to joust with the Queen's brother, landed at Gravesend is unknown, but the 'rich-apparailde' ships that lay off the town must have provided a delightful sight for its citizens.

Of those known to have been ashore with a great retinue, Cardinal Wolsey, who had met the Emperor Charles V of Spain at Dover with a train of earls, knights, bishops, abbots and chaplains, with 100 gentlemen and 700 yeomen, came to Gravesend where they embarked for Greenwich in 30 barges in 1522. Henry VIII, Wolsey's royal master, also landed in Gravesend from Erith in 1544, and having dined here, rode to Faversham for an expedition in France that he afterwards abandoned.

Sebastian Cabot, who 'banketted' with others at the *Christopher* inn (where the *Pier* hotel now stands) in 1556. Maybe also Martin Frobisher, who had a Gravesend man, James Bere, as his navigator on his second and third voyages in search of a north-west passage to China, and who with his crew 'received the Communion by the minister of Gravesend' board the *Ayde* in 1557.

Later royal personages included King Christian of Denmark, brother of James I's queen, ships of whose fleet lay off Gravesend in 1606 while he was on a visit which he repeated in 1614. On that occasion he was accompanied by Prince Henry, James's short-lived son; James II, who as Duke of York occupied a house where now is the western part of the *Clarendon* hotel, and who, in flight in 1688, landed and passed through the town; Charles I, both as prince and king, first *incognito* on a prospective matrimonial venture to Spain in 1623, and later with his bride, Queen Henrietta, in 1625; the Count Palatine of the Rhine, who landed at Gravesend in 1612 to espouse the Princess Elizabeth, daughter of James I, whose grandson was George I; and the Prince of Orange who, after his marriage with Princess Anne, daughter of George II, stayed in Gravesend, weather-bound, for three days in 1734.

To these royal persons may be added Andrew Marvell the poet, accompanying Lord Carlisle on a diplomatic mission to Muscovy, 1663; Pepys and John Evelyn, 1667; Hogarth, the painter, 1732; and John Wesley, 1734. A tablet formerly upon the Town Pier recorded the landing there in 1783 of August Strindberg, the Scandinavian playwright. The tablet is now in the local museum.

The beginnings of this part of the Thames shore as a landing-place lie beyond the reach of records.

The first rerefence is to be found in Domesday Book, that momumental inventory compiled under the authority of William the Conqueror, the date of which is given approximately as 1086–7. Here is to be found

> 'Herbert, son of Ivo, holds Gravesham of the Bishop . . . there is one church and one hythe . . .'

and

> 'Ralph, son of Thurold, holds of the Bishop, in the hundred of Toltingtrow, Meletune (Milton) . . . There is a church and 1 mill of 49 pence, and a hythe of 20 shillings, and 3 servants . . .'

As will have been realised, the Town Pier stands at the junction of the two parishes of Gravesend and Milton, and it has been thought by some that there being no value set upon the Gravesend hythe in Domesday, Milton bore the assessment of what was a common hythe of the two parishes. There may, however, have been a hythe in Gravesend parish, possibly the old landing place for the Cross Ferry at the Three Crowns Causeway. This adjoins the present ferry pontoon. The causeway beneath the old Town Pier may have been Milton's hythe.

3.—Gravesend tilt boat, 1753 (as used on Long Ferry)

What were the duties of the servants (the word used in Domesday is 'servi') can only be conjectured. That there was at that time a cross-river service to meet needs of the period can be taken as certain, and in all probability communication with London by river, later to be known as the 'Long Ferry' was already on a regularised footing. That a payment had to be made to the possessor of manorial rights suggests that this was obtainable from the traffic charges made and the revenue earned by the transport service. From the amount set down as the value of the hythe—20 shillings—some larger revenue than that arising from mere cross-river traffic may be assumed, and the Long Ferry would be likely to provide the bulk of the sum required.

Mention of the Long Ferry compels a brief treatment of the privileges which were conferred upon Gravesend watermen to whom were granted the sole right of conveying passengers by water between Gravesend and London. A royal grant of 1401 to this did not so much originate the privilege as confirm one that was already existent.

> We are informed that from time whereof the memory of man is not to the contrary, the Men of Gravesend . . . have been accustomed, and were used, without any interruption, freely quietly and peaceably to carry in their own vessels whatsoever persons coming to the town aforesaid, and willing to go thence by water to our city of London . . . that they in their own vessels, may for ever freely ship such persons coming to the said town of Gravesend and willing to go thence to our said city of London by water, etc

The Thames between the city of London and Gravesend was for centuries the highway taken by travellers proceeding farther into Kent, the roads out of London to the south-east being in bad condition and subjecting the traveller also to robbery by highwaymen. Those intending to proceed farther into Kent before the coming of stage-coaches did so by hiring horses from hackneymen; these having made their journeys returned to Gravesend and delivered up their steeds, which were all distinctly branded as a proof of ownership. The profession of 'hacqueneyeman' appears in local church registers.

The earliest mention of the landing-place after that in Domesday is in 1286 when on 2 June a violent storm seriously damaged 'the causeway and landing place'; and in 1293 complaint was made to the Justice of Assize of the dangerous condition of 'the bridge and chalk causeway leading to the water'. A decree was issued compelling the lord of the manor to repair the river moiety, and the men of Milton the land moiety. The terms 'bridge and chalk causeway' suggest that the approach to the river was by a raised platform of timber and that the foundation was a built-up base of chalk, square blocks of which material were employed as 'footings' of later buildings in the vicinity.

It is to be noted also that reference is made in the decree to the fact that due to the bad state of the bridge many 'both of our country and strangers are liable to suffer losses'. From this may be gathered that trading vessels from other countries were even at that time accustomed to moor off the town, their seamen landing at the bridge.

At the same assize certain boatmen of Gravesend were called to answer a charge that they had charged double the fare allowed in the statute which was one halfpenny for conveying a passenger to London. They craved mercy and were placed under a bond of forty shillings. How serious a penalty this was Pocock points out by stating that a halfpenny in 1293 was the equivalent of a shilling in purchasing power 400 years later.

The upkeep of the landing place over the next 400 years probably devolved upon the holders of the manor of Gravesend and upon the inhabitants of the town, a manorial record in 1360 referring to '128 pieces of elm timber to make piles for the new wharf'. The term 'wharf' suggests a built-up structure rather than the bridge or causeway of a century before.

When the town's Third Charter was granted in 1632 an annual sum of £6 14s. 4d. was fixed as payable to the Duke of Lennox as lord of the manor for the better maintenance of 'Gravesend and Milton Bridge'. This sum was paid until 1677 when it fell into abeyance for 15 years, at the end of which time the Corporation of the Borough put before the representative of the possessor of the manor that a sum of £115 13s. 9d. had been expended upon repairs to the bridge, whereupon the further payment of 'pontage' as it was called was excused and the Corporation became sole owners.

Little more is forthcoming regarding the structure of the quay until through the medium of Pocock's reporting, we learn that 'about 1765 the Town Stairs or Landing Place at the waterside was built of wood and often out of repair . . . To remedy this evil the Corporation in 1767 erected a spacious wharf with a crane &c to land goods, and made a substantial stone bridge or causeway . . . on this wharf are many sheds or shops which the Corporation let out mostly to gardeners, for the speedy supplying of ships'.

4.—Town Quay, *c.* 1800

Now that horses have all but disappeared from our streets, mention of the 'horse-wash' referred to in Corporation accounts, may require some explanation. It was the custom at the end of a day's work for draught horses to be ridden down into the river in the summer, where they refreshed themselves by splashing around: at the side of the quay a sloping descent was provided for this purpose. Another use is mentioned in accounts of the 17th century where under date 7 January 1636 payment was made to porters of 'two shillings for ducking of Goodwife Campion', this being carried out by strapping the unfortunate misdemeanant into a 'ducking stoole' and immersing her in the river.

The Town Pier (which was closed in 1969 when the passenger ferry was transferred to West Street Pier and the car ferry discontinued) was built in 1834 and opened by the Earl of Darley. Its construction was vigorously opposed by

5.—Fire at the *Pier* hotel, 1846. Town pier in the foreground

watermen of the period whose living depended to a large extent upon landing passengers from the steam vessels plying between Gravesend and London, and damage was caused to the early work undertaken to prepare for the building of the pier.

The pier was bought from the Corporation by the London, Tilbury and Southend Railway in 1885 and became their Gravesend station. It is now used as a restaurant.

The *Three Daws* on the east side of the Town Pier square is now the oldest public house in the town. Its many passages and stairs are said to have enabled sailors to escape the press gang and smugglers to ply their trade. By some miracle it escaped the many fires, in spite of its wooden construction. Its earlier name was the *Cornish Chough,* and before that the *Three Cornish Choughs.* In 1582 the innkeeper was Ralph Wellett. It seems to have been associated with pilgrims crossing the river on their way to the shrine of St. Thomas, the three Cornish Choughs appearing in the arms of Canterbury. A reference to it as the *Three Daws* appears in the Gravesend Register of 1667. Opposite, where now stands the *Pier* hotel, was the *Christopher*, referred to in a will of 1476. This public house or its successor was removed in 1828 when the Town Pier square was laid out. The *Pier* hotel was seriously damaged by the fire of 1846, when damage to the extent of £100,000 was done, and the Corporation at last established a proper fire brigade.

Chapter Four

WEST STREET AND CLIFTON MARINE PARADE

WEST STREET now presents a somewhat bleak appearance as a result of wholesale demolitions undertaken to widen the road to form the west-east route of the town's one-way system, and as a result of earlier slum clearance. It is now hard to picture it as it was as late as 1900, when its many shops competed with those of High Street for the custom of 'carriage folk', whose pair-horse broughams with liveried coachmen and footmen were to be seen drawn up at the grocer, the butcher, or the fishmonger, while the ladies from the large houses on the outskirts of the town made choice of bacon cuts, joints, or fish. In addition, on both sides of the street were shops with heaps of brown shrimps at twopence a pint, piled on clean white boards, the fruits of the labour of shrimpers, whose bawley-boats caught them and dispatched much of their catch to London shops and restaurants. Other shops specialised in herring, kippers and haddock smoked on the premises.

One great drawback of the street was its narrowness, in places only a carriage-width, besides which on its south side were the packed courts and alleys, many of them with wooden or lath and plaster houses in which the working-class men lived. Cesspool drainage with shared w.c.s and water from stand-pipes made this a most unhealthy area, frequently subject to cholera outbreaks in the middle and early years of the 19th century. A slum clearance scheme, strongly opposed by some of the inhabitants, was put into force in the 1920s and the area between West Street and Church Street has been completely cleared. Suttis Alley, St. John's Place, Pump Alley, Mermaid Court, Rawlinson's Place, Caroline Place and Passenger's Court have all gone. Only Chapel Lane, represented by a flagged pathway leading to St. George's church can now be traced. It was in Chapel Lane that Pocock informs us stood 'the oldest building in Gravesend'. He did not, however, enlarge on this statement beyond giving an illustration of one of its door lintels. In 1948, however, a baker's shop was demolished in West Street, and some 40ft. of ragstone wall standing about 13ft. high came to light parallel with Chapel Lane to the east and abutting to the south on the old Ragged School. Efforts by the local historical society to have this wall preserved were unsuccessful, but some photographs and a rough plan survive. There seems little doubt that this wall was the last remnant of the extensive manor house and chapel described in H.M. Stationery Office's *The History of the King's Works.* It was built by Edward III between 1362 and 1368, Bernard Cook being clerk of the works, at a cost of £1,350. The old wall appeared to have some pieces of Reigate stone as well as rag, and there are references in the accounts to this stone as well as chalk and flint. There are also references to a hall, chapel, kitchen, great gate, little gate, and park gate. In 1369-70 a new Wharf cost £39. In Buck's long view of the town (1738) there appears a small tower in this area which may well have been the remains of the 'great gate'. In 1376 Edward III transferred the manor to the Convent of St. Mary Graces, and they were authorised to use the materials from Gravesend for making a 'dormitory refectory cloister and other needfull buildings' for their convent, the 'East Minster', which stood on Tower Hill on the site lately occupied by The Mint.

West Street is probably nearly as old as High Street. It is mentioned as early as 1418 as 'West Street juxta Tamisam' and it may be that it was here that houses stood when in 1380 'certayn galeys of warre owt of France came to Gravysende and brente a grate part of the towne'.

The river side of the street had until a few years ago the distinction of possessing more licensed houses in its 400 yards length than any other street in the town. Many of these were survivals from the time when large sailing vessels were moored off the town awaiting supplies, and intending passengers, officers and crews together with their friends required refreshment and lodging ashore before the final 'farewell'. Later, some of these catered for visitors during Gravesend's prosperous years as a holiday resort, and a reminder of these times could until 1972 be seen from the river in the derelict glass-fronted dining-room of the *New Falcon* hotel, noted for its whitebait suppers and as the venue for mayoral banquets during the 19th century. It later became the New Falcon laundry, and was used for this purpose until about 1960.

Midway along the north side is the landing stage for the cross ferry between Tilbury and Gravesend. Until 1965 this was the landing-place for the car ferries. The last two boats were the *Mimie,* built in 1927, and the *Tessa,* in 1924. The opening of the Dartford tunnel rendered them obsolete. They had for some time been inadequate to deal with the summer traffic, when long queues formed waiting to cross the river. Their predecessors were the *Edith* and the *Gertrude,* built in 1911. At this period they were usually known as the cattle boats, as large flocks of sheep used to cross the river from Essex to the Kent markets. The earliest steam ferry seems to have been a chain ferry, which started in 1824. The present diesel passenger boats were introduced in 1960. Prior to that time the passenger service was operated by three steam boats, the *Rose,* built in 1901, the *Catherine,* in 1903, and the *Edith,* formerly used for cars and cattle. The *Rose* and the *Catherine* were the last passenger boats on the Board of Trade Register to be lit by oil lamps.

The beginnings of the cross ferry are difficult to determine. Pocock records (1797) that the Governor of Tilbury Fort 'claims the ferry from his premises to Gravesend on the same terms as the Corporation of Gravesend and Milton do theirs; and he built for the greater convenience of passengers a public house for his ferrymen to dwell on the spot'. This is the public house now known as *The World's End.* It may be assumed that led to a regular service between the *Three Crowns* landing stage, as it came to be known,and the *World's End* causeway on the Tilbury side. By the early 19th century the Gravesend departure place was known as the Ferry House. The Corporation and Government ferries were usually let to the same ferryman,and both were purchased by the London, Tilbury and Southend Railway in the 1880s.

Where Bath Street on the left joins West Street, now both part of the main traffic route, was a water gate or dock running into the land at this point. Cruden cites a deed of conveyance of 1567 whereby Robert Laiston, shipwright, acquires a property known as Spalding's Wharf in the west part of Gravesend (which abuts on the Thames to the north, on the water gate or dock on the east, on the Queen's Highway on the south, and on other property on the west). This would place the property just on the west side of Bath Street. Later, the dock and watercourse were covered in and known as Pipe Street.

Today at the foot of Bath Street is Metcalfe's wharf, where 70 years ago was Nettleingham's Steam Flour mills. Later, when the property was taken over by Pattullo, Higgs and Co., it was the spot at which some thousands of tons were nitrates were landed, at a time when the use of nitrates for fertilising agricultural land was widespread. Farther westwards, Russell's Gravesend Brewery (one of four local breweries which have all disappeared) together with its wharf covered a large area. Some of the buildings still remain and are used as a bottling store and a distributing centre for Truman's beer, although this is brewed elsewhere. A slipway on the right and Stuart Road on the left mark the end of West Street, and at this point Clifton Marine Parade is entered.

The viaduct overhead and the remains of West Street station are witness to hopes unrealised. Built by the London, Chatham and Dover Railway in 1886 to compete with the South Eastern line to the Central station it was originally intended to have a station nearer the High Street, but this was never built. It was closed for passenger traffic in 1953, although it continued to be used as the Gravesend goods depot until 1968, when it was closed completely. The pier was at one time used for a service to Clacton, and between 1916 and 1939 for the Batavier service to Rotterdam, during which time the line had a 'boat train'.

About 70 feet to the west of the viaduct were discovered in 1910 the skeletons of two male persons in chains, and in 1957 further skeletons were found in the vicinity. It was probably in this area that a gibbet stood on which malefactors were hung, as Pocock also records in 1796 the finding of two men buried in chains at the west end of the

Rope Walk which ran above the later Clifton Marine Parade on the north side. Iron manacles found near the site of the gibbet are now in the local museum.

In Gravesend's prosperous period as a health resort, the Clifton Marine Parade was a pleasant promenade, and except for a short length at its western end where waggons crossed the road to load chalk into waiting sailing ships, provided an undershore walk with open views of the river all along the way to Northfleet. This pleasant prospect was ended when the whole of the land upon its south side was acquired by the Imperial Paper Mills Ltd. in 1910, in order to erect huge mills and include storage room for pulp and other requirements of paper-making. On the river side the view of the river was obstructed by the construction of wharves and buildings thereon.

In 1796 bathing-machines were first used upon the foreshore, with the Clifton baths at the rear, and in 1837 they were rebuilt in pseudo-Oriental architecture. They provided swimming facilities, separate for each sex, hot and tepid baths for the languid; while the Royal Thames Yacht Club, formerly *Pallister's* hotel, was the centre of considerable yachting activities: King Edward VII when Prince of Wales was a frequent visitor. Seats were provided for visitors in front of the baths where, to quote a chronicler of 1864, 'the convalescent may enjoy an animated view of the river and the scenery of the opposite coast', which was at that time open marshland, Tilbury Docks not being constructed until the middle years of the 1880s.

Just within the Parade at its eastern end was an ascending road leading to an extensive rope-walk, and some distance farther the dwelling-house of its proprietor, Alderman Ditchburn, which could also be approached from the Parade by means of a stairway. Just beyond the stairway was the garden of the quaintly-named *Hit or Miss*, whose name has provided a mass of conjectures. It certainly had this name in 1805. Hereabouts in the 17th century was a municipal bowling-green held in the name of the Corporation of the time, and here later, when the ground had been excavated for chalk, was a rifle range for Volunteer regiments in the 1860s. Either of these uses may have provided the inn with its name. The present public house was built on the site in 1929.

Near the Gravesend boundary, where now pulp ships are unloaded at a pier, there was in the late 18th and early 19th century the shipbuilding yards and slips of William Cleverly, who built there a number of warships and merchant vessels, up to nearly 2,000 tons, these, of course, being sailing ships. Shipbuilding was continued here by William's grandson Henry, who subsequently found a better source of profit in lime-burning and providing chalk ballast for coasting ships bringing coal from northern ports into London river.

Lime-burning provided a return to an activity which existed in Gravesend in the 17th century. Cruden, citing a document in 1696, which gives details of profits of lime-burning, with the note that when Mr. Etkins had these cliffs Mr. Stanbrook had three kilns going and Mr. Marshall two. Entries of deaths of chalk-diggers and lime-burners are in local church registers.

The business of chalk shipping and lime-burning was later carried on by Lieut.-Col. Gladdish, connected with the Cleverlys by marriage, and later still by William Fletcher, both of whom resided in a house, 'Bycliffes', near the wharves, which was built by William Cleverly. Beneath the cliffs was a row of cottages, known as Slaves Alley, in which the 'chalkies' lived.

The Northfleet boundary adjoins Gravesend at the point where the road rises, and so closes this chapter on West Street and its continuation, Clifton Marine Parade.

From this point we return to visit St. George's church.

Chapter Five

ST. GEORGE'S CHURCH

THE CHURCH of St. George was visible from West Street, and as we return from the journey described in the last chapter, we will turn up Bath Street and into Church Street to make our way to the church, passing on our right Church Street school, the first 'board school' to be built in the town in 1876. The present church was built in 1731 on the site of an earlier church, built about 1480, and destroyed by fire in 1727 (see Chapter Two, p. 13). The pre-Conquest parish church of Gravesend is presumed to have stood, as did its successor, on a piece of ground between half and three-quarters of a mile to the south-west (see Chapter Thirteen). St. George's was licensed for saying Mass on 22 April 1497, and consecrated on 2 April 1510 by Bishop Fisher. On the same day he re-dedicated the church of St. Mary after its destruction or damage by fire.

The chapel of ease or oratory, dedicated to St. George, was constituted the parish church in 1544: the reasons set out in the Letters Patent were that the church of St. Mary was at so great a distance from the town that infirm people, pregnant women, and others, found great inconvenience in attending. From contemporary records it would seem that St. Mary's church had already fallen into decay, and the last burial in its graveyard was in 1598.

What the first St. George's church looked like is unknown as no illustration survives. We can, however, gather from vestry notes that it had a wooden steeple which was in poor condition in 1719, being just a case of boards, and from Thorpe that it contained a number of memorials, including a rhymed inscription in memory of James Bere, the navigator of Frobisher's ships, and consisted of a chancel, nave, north aisle and 'handsome' vestry room. There was also a brass sconce left by David Varchell. All the church furniture, including this memorial, were destroyed in the fire of 1727.

6.—St. George's church, *c.* 1840

Faced with the need to build a new church the Corporation, supported by the local vestry, sought the aid of Parliament under the Act of 1714 of Queen Anne for building 50 new churches by means of a grant out of accumulated funds produced by a tax on coal entering the Port of London. This was more successful than an earlier application for a grant under the Act to effect repairs to the earlier church and rebuild its steeple in brick and stone.

A grant of £5,000 was obtained through a Private Act of Parliament from the source above mentioned. This enabled work to be put in hand under the direction of Charles Sloane, a local architect, a tablet to whose memory is still to be seen on the west wall of the church. The foundation stone was laid on 3 June 1731, and the church was opened on 11 February 1733. During the interim Divine Services were held in the Town Hall.

The fact that the church was built from the coal tax was commemorated in the following verse:

This Fabrick which at first was built
To be God's House of Pray'r
And not to pamper Priests of Guilt
Or hold a sleeping Mayor
Once perish'd by the vengeful Flame
Which all its beauties raz'd
Nor could the awful Patron's name
Protect the Pile it graced
But as it fell before the Fire
Which then destroyed it whole
So now to Heav'n its heights aspire
And rise again by Coal.

The Corporation of Gravesend organised a scheme for providing a peal of bells by private subscription. Eight bells were hung, inscribed with the names of those subscribing, and during the next 100 years or so they were rung on every possible occasion, not only on national days of importance, but whenever important personalities, English or foreign, passed down the river aboardship.

The church today contains a number of wall memorials and stained glass windows in honour of local 19th-century celebrities. There is also in the churchyard a bronze statue of Princess Pocahontas, presented by the people of Virginia and unveiled by the Governor of Virginia on 5 October 1958. Pocahontas was the daughter of the Red Indian chief, Powhattan, whose courage saved the life of the English captain, John Smith, when her father planned to kill him. She probably died on board a ship in the river in 1616 and was buried beneath the chancel of the older church, and in 1914 two windows were inserted at the east end of the church on either side of the chancel and filled with stained glass by the Colonial Dames of Virginia. United States visitors come to the church during the summer months to inspect the windows, which have in addition to the large figures of Rebecca (Pocahontas's Christian name) and Ruth (the biblical personality who left her Moabite home to dwell in Israel), small representations of Pocahontas from contemporary sources. On the west wall is a framed facsimile of the entry in the burial register of 1616, reading:

> *May 1616.*
>
> Rebecca Wrothe, wyffe of Thomas Wrothe, gent. a Virginia Lady borne, was buried in ye Chauncell.

Among other memorials is one to General Gordon, who was a resident of Gravesend while he was Commanding Royal Engineer in the district.

When the church was built a gallery ran along the north side, the pulpit being opposite where the war memorial is now. The west gallery and organ were purchased in 1764 by a legacy left by John Ison, who owned the *Catherine Wheel* in High Street. In 1818 a south gallery was added and the pulpit moved into the centre of the church, and in 1833 upper galleries were added at the west end, the outlines of which can be seen on either side of the old organ. In 1892 the chancel was extended, and in 1897 the north aisle built by Basset-Smith, and all the galleries removed except the west one. When the church was closed in 1952 and St. James became the parish church, the north side was converted into a flat by Mr. G. Tatchell, the honorary custodian, and the church used as a Chapel of Unity and Mayor's Chapel. In 1962 it was re-opened as a church to replace Holy Trinity, and in 1968 became the parish church once more. In 1970 the north aisle was again re-opened and a new organ built, and the church restored chairs, replacing the open sittings (installed in 1872 to replace the original pews). When the work was carried out four column bases were found which had been used for the north gallery supports, apparently from the old church.

In Church Street, the thoroughfare north of the church, there stood for many years the Ragged School, built in 1862 to replace the original Ragged School, started in a wooden shed in the Old Main (Clifton Road) in 1851. In course of time a Penny Bank, a Free Day school, Mother's Meeting, shoeblack brigade, and soup kitchen were carried on for the benefit of the dwellers in the courts and alleys in the neighbourhood. Its activities were transferred to a new housing estate at Denton, where, under the title of the

Gordon Mission (in memory of General Gordon, who was one of the many voluntary helpers in the Church Street premises) it carries on religious and social work in more encouraging circumstances.

Although it has disappeared as a public thoroughfare, Chapel Lane calls for mention here. It was a wide-paved footway with dwelling-houses on both sides, leading from West Street to Church Street, where it issued nearly opposite the churchyard gates. There is reason to suspect that Chapel Lane was originally church property as several entries in the Vestry accounts in the 18th and 19th centuries record payments for repair made out of church rates. The name is thought to go back to the end of the 15th century when St. George's was built as a chapel of ease. A house on the south-west corner was for some years after 1800 the post office of the town.

Along Church Street on Friday, 16 June 1797, the body of William Wallace, one of the mutineers who had taken a leading part in the Mutiny of the Nore, and had shot himself upon its failure, was taken from the belfry of the church where it had lain for inquest, exposed to the view of the populace at the church gate, and then taken on a low carriage via Bath Street, West Street, High Street, to cross roads near the junction of Darnley Road and Old Road, where it was buried with a stake driven between the thighs according to the custom of the time.

Chapter Six

BATH STREET, STUART ROAD AND PRINCES STREET

RETURNING ALONG Church Street westwards, we pass Kempthorne Street (now devoid of houses except for the new rectory and church hall opened in 1970), which owes its name to a lady who became the wife of John Wakefield, and to whose memory a table tomb with an epitaph in verse once stood at the south-west corner of the churchyard. Her father, Thomas Kempthorne, was a Commissioner of the Navy, and was stationed at Chatham. Her husband, whose name is perpetuated in Wakefield Street, was earlier a waiter at the *King's Head*, Gloucester. Mrs. Wakefield died in 1772.

Bath Street was the road which lead to the Clifton baths, hence the name, and before turning southwards the last remaining portion of the former highway, to Northfleet must be noted opposite. This was the main road to Northfleet, cut in 1716 to replace an earlier road nearer the river: it became dangerous by being cut into for chalk needed for ballast for ships, and for lime-burning, and was replaced by the present New Road–Overcliffe, in 1802. It was still known as the Old Main (Road) in 1900, although its official name was changed to Clifton Road. A small cottage which stood on the south-east corner of this road until 1950 was used for the first Ragged School and was the last thatched house in the town. There is an illustration of it in the Library Collection.

The first gas works, established in 1824, was on the west side of Bath Street, just south of the Old Main until 1843, in which year they were removed to the banks of the Thames and Medway Canal at the east end of the town, where, extended and improved, the plant was operated by the South Eastern Gas Board until 1958. The town was first lighted by gas on 9 December 1824.

Stuart Road embodies one of the names of the Darnley family, and when the railway was opened the road was claimed as a private road and barred under his lordship's orders. The barriers were broken down by employees of the company, and legal steps threatened, but the differences between the parties were settled without resort to law.

Between Bath Street and Stuart Road is the Gravesend and North Kent hospital which, since 1948, has been administered under the National Health Service. This hospital, opened in 1854, had its origin in the gift of a site by the Earl of Darnley in 1853. The first dispensary in the town was opened on 2 December 1850 at 89 (later 133) Milton Road, at the corner of Wellington Street, its object being 'to assist the really destitute poor of Gravesend and Milton and vicinities . . . unable to pay for medical aid'. Until 1948 the hospital was conducted on a voluntary basis. The well-known hospital fetes at Rosherville Gardens and elsewhere as well as industries, private individuals and friendly societies provided financial support.

A description of the hospital in *Jottings of Kent,* 1864, under the title of 'Gravesend Dispensary and Infirmary' is given here to provide a contrast with the hospital as it is today.

> This substantial building of brick approached by a flight of stone steps under a near portico, is divided in two parts, the front portion being the Dispensary, comprising waiting and consulting rooms, the surgery and the private residence of the indefatigable house surgeon; here sick poor, not receiving parish relief, have medical aid and medicines for one penny . . . The Dispensary has beds for twenty patients; on an average there are from six to ten under treatment in the Infirmary, and upwards of one hundred weekly in the Dispensary.

N. C. H. Nisbett was the Architect of the new building of 1895. The hospital has recently been greatly extended and the new block was opened in 1971.

About 50 yards down Bath Street from New Road on its eastern side there stood until 1834 a small National school, but in that year it joined forces with the Free school in King Street (see Chapter Eight) under a scheme for joint management.

At the eastern side of the square formed by Church Street, Bath Street and New Road (see Chapter Eight) is Princes Street, known earlier as Princess Street, and earlier still as Bread Street and Gravesend Backside.

Princes Street was associated for many years with Congregational or Independent worship. The chapel was closed in 1953 and its congregation now meets in the Old Road East in what was formerly a large private house. A meeting-house and burial ground and minister's house were built in 1717, with help from London Dissenters. This was enlarged in 1797 and rebuilt in 1838. John Gould, a well-known local architect-builder, who lived in Princes Street, was clerk of works of the 1838 Princes Street chapel. Extensions in 1860 and 1879 included lecture hall, schoolroom and library. The first Sunday School in the town was started by this church in 1801 in a room in Swan Alley. The building was finally demolished in 1961, the site now being occupied by a car park.

Chapter Seven

OVERCLIFFE AND ROADS ON ITS SOUTH SIDE

CHAPTER FOUR of this Guide brought our peregrinations at its close to the Northfleet boundary by the riverside. Our starting point now is directly south of the riverside boundary where Gravesend joins Northfleet on the road cut by the Turnpike Commissioners in 1801, mentioned in Chapter Six. This section of the road between Northfleet and New Road is known as Overcliffe, formerly spelt without the final 'e'. The first houses, built about 1835, were those on the north side, identified for many years as Darnley Terrace. They were demolished about 1953 and the site is now occupied by a garage. At the time they were built the surrounding ground had not been cut away, and there was pastureland on both sides and at the rear level with the gardens. This formed part of the old Fairfield which stretched to Bath Street, and where the annual Gravesend Fair was held. This was excavated during the years which followed, until late in the 19th century almost all the old Fairfield had disappeared. Until the acquisition of the quarry in 1910–11 by the Imperial Paper Mills, two lime kilns stood in the quarry at the back of Darnley Terrace, their glow when lime-burning was being conducted lighting up the foliage of trees around with an 'Inferno' glare. In spite of the commercialisation of the quarry, nightingales sang there until just before the end of the 19th century.

The residences on the south side of Overcliffe were built at varying times from 1864 onwards until 1870 and were provided with deep gardens behind which was pastureland extending back to Pelham Road and cut only by the railway which runs obliquely in a north-easterly direction to Gravesend Central station. This land was known as Mr. Cove's field in the early 19th century, a cottage with an orchard towards the eastern end of Overcliffe, between St. James's Street and St. James's Avenue, being known as 'Cove's Cottage'.

Upon part of the pastureland, Gravesend Cattle Fair was held in the early 1890s when the old Fairfield had been so reduced as to make it too small for that purpose. In 1893 the northern part, where now is Lennox Avenue, was fenced in with corrugated iron sheeting set vertically to provide an enclosure for the newly-formed Gravesend United Football Club, itself the result of the joining of forces and interests by the Gravesend Football Club and Gravesend Ormonde, the latter largely composed of Gravesend watermen. The ground was entered from Overcliffe over a semi-public cart-track from Overcliffe to Pelham Road, which was closed during football matches despite public objection. Just on the north of the railway bridge were cowhouses and milking sheds of a dairyman and cowkeeper named Cackett, whose name still adheres to the bridge leading to Grange Road, which figures as Cackett's Bridge in local minds. The site of St. James's Avenue was Cackett's Meadow. The houses in Lennox Avenue and St. James's Avenue were erected between 1910 and 1919.

Lennox Road was cut in 1877: before that time there was no road for vehicles between Darnley Road and Dover Road, Northfleet, except for the cart-track above-mentioned. For some years, Lennox Road was popularly known as the 'New Cut', and was much used by persons learning the popular new art of 'bicycling'.

The larger houses in Overcliffe, east of St. James's Avenue, all had long gardens opening upon what is now St. James's Road (many of these have now been shortened and houses built, which front on to the latter road). At its western end, St. James's Road petered out into a nursery with large glasshouses, the proprietor being one named Spicer. All this area was formerly included in the 40-acre Fairfield.

The three houses in a block, Nos. 6, 7 and 8 Overcliffe, now the Gravesend Art School, were earlier private houses.

The Overcliffe on its north side, with its wide flagged pavement was an attractive promenade: before the present century it had only an asphalt patched footway bordered by a broken quick hedge. Buses of the Maidstone and District Company, with services to large areas of Kent and Sussex, occupy much of the roadway at busy times; the company's booking offices and garages built in 1923 stand upon the last remaining patch of the old cattle fairground. This site gave much trouble due to cliff falls, until a concrete retaining wall was built.

The first Maidstone and District bus service to Chatham started in 1911. In 1923 they took over the services which the Tramway Company had started in 1913. The first motor buses in the town were two small 12-seaters operated by Messrs. Smith and Day between Gravesend and Northfleet between July 1901 and August 1902, while the tramway was being relayed for electric operation.

Chapter Eight

NEW ROAD AND KING STREET

NEW ROAD is that section of the main thoroughfare which extends from Stuart Road to the top of High Street. The first building on the north side, proceeding from Overcliffe (now a furniture emporium) was from 1855 to 1937 St. James's church day school, having a stone wall adjoining the path enclosing the now open square as a forecourt. The shops adjoining are among the oldest in the road, having been built as dwelling-houses in the early years of the 19th century. The large building now unoccupied, lately used as a shop and formerly the Super cinema, was built in 1880 as the Borough of Gravesend British Workman's Halls. It then became the Gravesend Public Halls and was used for meetings, lectures, concerts and entertainments. An upper hall, smaller in size, was used for social functions. It was here that films were first regularly shown, when the hall was given the name of the Popular Picture Palace in 1912.

From 1852 to 1968 there stood at the corner of Darnley Road the church of St. James. It was the first building to be erected on the land south of the New Road and west of Darnley Road. It was built at a cost of £3,400 under the Church Building Act of 1818 with a small grant of £300. S. W. Dawkes was the architect, and the style was decorated Gothic. It was built of Kentish ragstone (which stood up to the weather better than the rag at either Holy Trinity or Rosherville) and slated. It was cruciform and had a very large square central tower which gave it somewhat the effect of a toy fort. The nave was not much larger than the transepts. The church was said to have been modelled on Poynings in Sussex. When it was demolished in 1968 the very fine stained glass east window of the crucifixion, by Wiliment, went to the Victoria and Albert Museum, and the oak altar (which dated from 1953) went to Cobham. The site was presented by the Earl of Darnley, and the church's

7.–St. James's church, *c.*1860

first incumbent was the Rev. John Joynes, whose brothers and father had been, or were, incumbents of local churches. It originally had galleries in both transepts, but these darkened the church so much that they were removed. The clock in the tower was presented in memory of Captain Marsden, a former harbour-master and a worshipper at the church. Between 1952 and 1968 it was the parish church of Gravesend.

Irregular roofs and upper storeys still existing at the western end of New Road serve to remind us that when the road was first constructed it was largely a road of small cottage dwellings, some of which on the southern side stood behind iron railings which remained until the closing years of the 19th century, when the houses were converted into shops. The *Sun* public house stood until 1970 at the corner of Bath Street, and until 1928 *The New Prince of Orange,* built in a similar style stood at the corner of High Street. They may be compared with the chemist's shop formerly at the top of Princes Street. They were all of the same style of architecture, built of local stock bricks and slated with mansard roofs and dated from the early 19th century, when New Road was cut.

On the south side of the road at the corner of Garrick Street, the long, low building which flanks that street, now a seedsman's store, was used in the early 19th century as a stable and coach-house for some of the coaches plying between Gravesend and London.

At the corner of Garrick Street stood the Theatre Royal, later the Salvation Army citadel. The Theatre Royal was opened for the presentation of plays in 1807 by Mr. J. Trotter. It suffered many fluctuations of fortune, being closed and then re-opened in 1822. Another period of varying fortune followed, and it appears to have reached its greatest height of popularity in the 1870s, but it declined again in public favour and was bought by the Salvation Army in 1883. Its new owners removed the two-tier balcony and made other alterations to fit it for its new role. It was demolished in 1969. At the same time the *Eagle* public house and a builder's merchant's yard adjoining, which was formerly the Royal mews; one of the leading livery and bait stables in the town was also demolished.

The two private houses standing back from the road with long gardens in front were demolished in 1958 to provide a site for the Co-operative store. These two houses were formerly occupied by Dr. Charles Pinching, the third and last generation of a family of Gravesend doctors who had originally lived on the Terrace. The western one of this pair of houses was at one time the offices and printing works of the *Gravesend and Northfleet Standard,* which flourished for a few years towards the close of the 19th century.

The premises demolished in 1973, occupied by Lloyds Bank, were built in 1906 by Alfred Tolhurst as offices for his firm and as a branch of the Capital and Counties Bank. (Architect, George E. Clay.) They occupied the site of earlier offices built in 1867 and a small public house. Behind it was an oblique path which at the beginning of the 19th century led to a nursery garden which gave the name to Garden Row next to the offices just mentioned. The nurseryman's residence, a wooden building, was later the stationmaster's house, and then used as a builders' office, pulled down in 1971.

The Midland Bank branch stands on ground that for many years was a stonemason's yard, first in the occupation of one Brisley, but from 1830 until 1900 the business was conducted by Charles Steel and his son, who died in that year. At one time negotiations were afoot for building a cinema on the site, but these fell through, and the bank bought the area and erected the present dignified building. The architect was T. B. Whinney.

In the 1830s No. 81 was the post office of the town, but in 1842 the office was removed to the corner of Edwin Street.

The section of New Road between Princes Street and High Street and between Stone Street and Windmill Street was from 1801 until the coming of the railway in 1849 the most lively in the town. Here the coaches plying between Faversham, Canterbury, Dover and London, halted to pick up and set down passengers, and to change horses. Pocock speaks of 17 coaches each way each day, so there must have

8.—New Road, top of High Street, with coaches at *The New Prince of Orange* and *Nelson, c.* 1835

been almost continuous traffic at this point. *The New Prince of Orange* with its 'tap' occupied the whole of the road on the north side, the *Nelson* that same length on the south side.

An announcement of 1840 speaks of the 'Nelson' from Brompton arriving at the *Lord Nelson* at 8 a.m.; the 'Commodore', also from Brompton at 10.30, stopping at *The Prince of Orange* on its way to the *Spread Eagle,* Gracechurch Street; the 'Tantivy' from Faversham, disposing of its Gravesend passengers at the *Nelson* and *The Prince of Orange* on alternate days, with the *Blossoms* inn, Lawrence Lane, as its destination; the 'Mail' every day at a quarter to two; the 'Eagle' and 'Union' from Dover at 3.30 and 4.30 to the *White Bear,* Piccadilly; the 'Express' from Dover at 4.30 for the *Golden Cross,* Westminster; the 'Tally-ho' from Canterbury at 7 p.m. for the *Spread Eagle,* Gracechurch Street; the 'Eagle' and 'Union' from Dover at 2 a.m.; and the 'Mail' at the same hour.

On the return journey the 'Nelson' arrived from London every evening at 8 p.m.; the others throughout day, the last being the 'Union' at 12.30 p.m.

In addition an omnibus ran from the *Nelson* daily to Meopham, Wrotham and Ightham, and a coach arrived from Maidstone every morning in time to catch the 8 a.m. boat to London in the years following 1815, when the first steamboat undertook regular services to London. It also waited to pick up passengers from the boat when they returned from London in the evening.

The *Nelson* hotel in the days of the coaches, and, indeed, until as late as 1878, had a balcony overlooking the street from which departing passengers could be waved 'farewell'. The hotel front was reconstructed in the year mentioned and the balcony removed and the road widened.

Readers who have followed the preceding chapters will realise that our steps have now led us around the outside of a square (with an excursion along the former Clifton Marine Parade) since we began in Chapter Two our entry into High Street. Proceeding eastwards we now enter King Street.

King Street was known until the late 18th century as St. Thomas's Street (see above, Chapter Two), and on a site now occupied by Barclays Bank and Abbey National there stood until 1928 the King Street school, and its predecessor, the old Free school. In his *St. George's School, Gravesend, 1580–1955* the late Mr. D. W. Jenkins describes the school thus:

> The school itself was a wooden building, about 60 feet long which faced south. There was a gable at one end and a dormer window at the other. The second storey overhung the ground floor and was lighted by a window which ran the whole length of the building. Very possibly the schoolroom was on this floor, while the schoolmaster lived on the ground floor.

Exactly when the school was built is unknown, but as early as 1580 the school was in being and was then situated, so it is believed, near the market place, that is between High

9.—Old Free School, *c.* 1800

Street and Queen Street. It was probably removed to the St. Thomas's Street site early in the 17th century.

When, in 1835, it was decided to join forces with the National school, which had been started in 1817, the old building was demolished and a new school erected with a front owing something to the design of one of the wings of Cobham Hall, whose owner, Lord Darnley, was Hereditary High Steward of Gravesend. The boys' department was on the ground floor, and the girls' school above.

This school remained in being as a church school until 1928, and in February 1939 a new St. George's school was opened off Upper Wrotham Road (see Chapter Fourteen), and the premises were sold for commercial purposes.

At the corner of Queen Street there stood until 1971 *The Mitre* which was intended to be known as the *Duke of York*: what influenced the change in name is not clear. With the cottage adjoining it was a pleasant red brick building with a dentil cornice and the last remaining building of this period in King Street.

The south side of the street was of later development. Until well into the 19th century the wall of a garden of a house whose entrance was in Parrock Street (now the

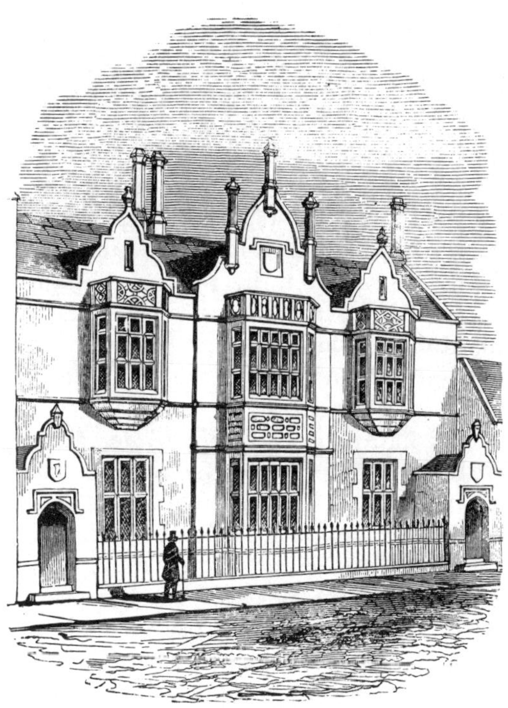

10.—King Street school, *c.* 1835

Conservative Club) ran along a length of the street on that side. Nearer Windmill Street on the same side are the County Court offices, built in 1878, and now used for the Crown Court. The National Westminster Bank (1898) and David Greig's (1903) were built on the site of the almshouses. In front of these almshouses was the cab rank in the 19th century. In the late 19th and early 20th centuries it was customary to station a long-extending fire-ladder on two large wheels outside the bank in King Street each night in case of emergency.

Chapter Nine

QUEEN STREET, EAST STREET AND HARMER STREET

IT IS PROPOSED in the first part of this chapter to complete the square of which Chapters Two and Eight on High Street and King Street cover the west and south sides. Our starting-point is where King Street (dealt with in the last chapter) leads into Milton Road and is crossed by Parrock Street and Queen Street. Turning to the left we descend Queen Street towards the river.

This street was known in the early 18th century as Milton Backside, as Princes Street was Gravesend Backside, the street backing upon the High Street. It is probable that from early times a trackway or bridle path led from the Town Quay along the present line of the street. When an Act for paving streets in Gravesend was passed in 1773, Queen Street was not among those named, but in the Milton Highway Surveyors' Accounts for 1806 there are payments for 'paviors' work in Queen Street' and a bill for 36 tons of pebbles laid down there.

On the right as we descend the street there is a space at the rear of the *New* inn (which is dealt with in the chapter on Milton Road), which was in the latter part of the 19th century a busy livery and bait stable conducted by Richard Turner. In addition to the provision of hack horses, carriages and three-and four-horse waggonettes for hire, the proprietor had always available for emergencies horses to be harnessed into the town's fire brigade vehicles upon an alarm being sounded.

Adjoining the stables was one of the half-dozen or so blacksmith's forges of the town, the chief business of which was the shoeing of the numerous horses employed in various forms of transport. This forge was carried on by one Vaughan. It may be noted here that the last farrier to carry on business in the town, and who devoted himself in the intervals of shoeing and wheelwright's work to the

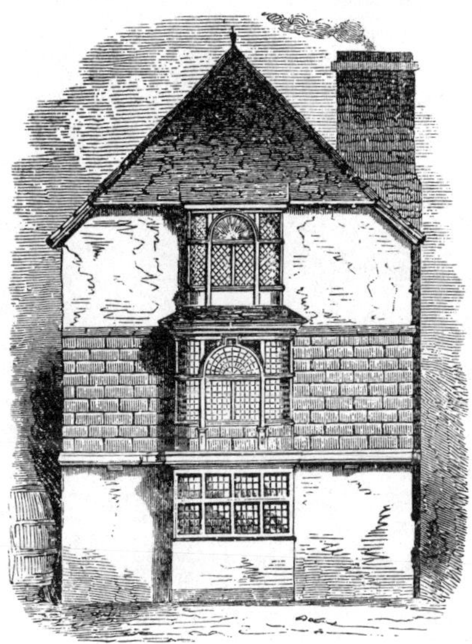

11.–Etkins House, *c.* 1840

production of artistic ornamental scroll work in metal was Wm. Harpum. His forge was on the opposite side of the street a few yards lower down and closed in 1960. It had been in his family since 1906. Some of his ornamental ironwork can be seen in Milton church.

Some newly-erected shops on the left-hand side of the street about 40 yards down stand upon the site of a house demolished in 1951, which was believed by many to be the residence of George Etkins, Sheriff of Kent in 1681, and owner of the Manor of Parrock until he disposed of it to the Corporation of Gravesend in 1694. Cruden speaks of Etkins's house as being on the west side of Queen Street and identifies the site more closely as being on the south side of Anchor and Crown Yard. The *Anchor and Crown* public house was in a direct line with the house. Before its demolition the upper storey had been altered, but experts declared it to be about 300 years old, and the demolition revealed that it was erected upon oak posts nearly a foot square and 20 feet or so in length, with the bark still adhering on the unworked side, and with the butts of the posts at the upper end.

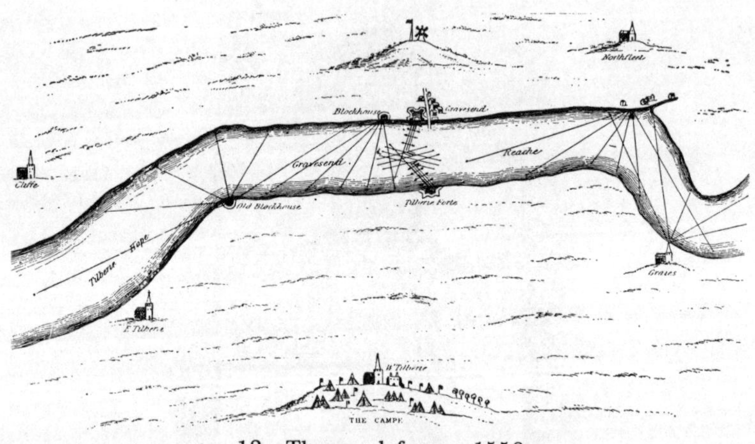

12.—Thames defences, 1558

About 70 yards lower down is the east end of the market (see Chapter Two) and opposite it on the right side is Terrace Street, at the corner of which is the *George* inn, the only one now left of four—the *Rose of Denmark,* the *Roebuck* and the *Ordnance Arms.* Demolition and the construction of the new ring road have completely altered the appearance of the lower part of the street known as Crooked Lane. It was a narrow, short street of sharp turns, where common lodging houses were situated. The *Ordnance Arms* on the right which was behind a cobbled space derived its name from the time when the land around belonged to the War Department, Henry VIII having built a blockhouse by the waterside below this point. Behind the *Ordnance Arms* was Sussex Place, a pleasant row of cottages largely inhabited by waterside workers, with gardens in front, reminiscent of the time when it was imperative for watermen to live near their work. Thames House at the end of Sussex Place still survives, now used as an annexe to the *Clarendon* hotel.

The opportunity has been taken since the removal of the old houses to open up this part of the riverside and plant it with shrubs so as to make it a smaller promenade. Turning towards the former Town Pier, dealt with in Chapter Three we cross what was known for centuries

1. New Road, *c.*1890. (See page 43)

2. Clifton Marine Parade, 1895. Clifton Shades, Royal Thames Yacht Club and Clifton Baths at the time of the great frost. (See page 27)

3. Holy Trinity church, *c.* 1880. Ordnance Road is on the right. (See page 67)

4. Christ Church, *c.* 1880. Note the change in colour in stone of the 1864 extensions. (See page 99)

5. Singlewell Road, *c.* 1880, taken from a point near the present Central Parade of shops. Note the old *Prince of Orange* and houses in Old Road East but none in Old Road West, Singlewell Road or Cross Lane, which is the hedge in the middle distance. (See page 111)

6. Portland Villas, Windmill Street, *c.* 1903. Note the tram en route for the *Prince of Orange.* (See page 103)

7. The Windmill and Belle Vue Tavern, *c.*1880. (See page 3)

8. Shrimpers at Bawley Bay, *c.*1870. (See page 51)

9. The River and St. George's tower, *c.* 1950. Taken from the tower of St. James' church. The *Sun* is in the foreground, and the roofs of houses in Bath Street and Wakefield Street, all now demolished, are visible. (See page 42)

10. Passengers Court, *c.* 1925. (See page 23)

11. King Street, *c.* 1895. Note the Almshouses and cab rank. (See page 47)

12. Boorman's Mill (Rural Vale), *c.* 1900. From a water-colour by J. S. Kean. (See page 135)

13. Rosherville Gardens, *c.* 1880, the Rose Garden and terrace. (See page 131)

14. The Hill, Northfleet, *c.* 1895. (See page 137)

15. Gravesend Piers, *c.*1902. The 'Rose' screw-ferry at Town Pier and probably 'Cato' paddle ferry at West Street Pier. (See page 20)

16. Northfleet High Street, *c.*1900. Note the horse tramway terminus. (See page 142)

as East Street. Prior to a fire in 1857, East Street was barely more than carriage width, and the destruction of houses at the bottom of High Street enabled the Commissioners to widen it somewhat by taking the old Star steamship building site into the roadway.

Like West Street, East Street had its share of licensed houses. In addition to the *Three Daws* there was the *Old Falcon,* the *King of Prussia* (whose title was changed to the *King of the Belgians* soon after the outbreak of the 1914–18 war), and the *Old Amsterdam* (where the Corporation banquets were held, and which is referred to in the well-known song), while a few yards farther on a site now occupied by St. Andrew's Waterside church, was the *Spread Eagle,* part of the old house still remaining. Set between them there was for a great many years during the latter part of the 19th century, the boat-building premises of Bill Warner, where during slack times watermen gathered to converse with the builder on football and politics, upon both of which subjects he held strong opinions. The business was continued later by his son, until just after the 1939–45 war. Wood's brewery, formerly Beckett's, occupied a site on the riverside here. There was also the dwelling-house of the owner of the brewery, and beyond these was a coalyard owned for many years by Edward Bannister and Co. The site, which included a number of old weather-boarded buildings, was cleared in 1954. The area is now covered by the pleasant enclosed greensward, provided with seats for residents and visitors.

The foreshore around St. Andrew's Waterside Mission church is generally known as Bawley Bay, this being formerly the moorings of the shrimping boats, called 'bawleys', of which there were large numbers during the 19th century. From about 1920 motor-boats were used, and the last shrimper to use this mooring belonged to Ted Burbury, who retired in 1965. The bay on the west side of the church is Blockhouse dock: the whole area came within the blockhouse property before it was disposed of in 1835. The actual blockhouse building, erected in the reign of Henry VIII, occupied a site on the east side of the *Clarendon* lawn, now occupied by the car park. The

Gravesend blockhouse has recently been excavated and the foundations of an ashlar bastion found.

Opposite the church there was until shortly after the Second World War a row of fishermen's cottages, known officially as Thames Terrace, but colloquially as Bawley Row. A boatbuilder, Waters's, was at the western end.

St. Andrew's Waterside Mission church was built in 1870 as a place of worship for the waterside fraternity. The architect was G. E. Street. It was a daughter church of Holy Trinity, Milton (see Chapter Eleven), and its registers contain records of the baptisms by the clergy of the church of emigrants awaiting departure to Australia and New Zealand in the 1860s and 1870s, when the voyages were attended by the dangers which sailing-ships were exposed to in those southern seas.

St. Andrew's church had its origin in the devotion of the Rev. C. E. R. Robinson, a former vicar of Holy Trinity, who made it part of his duties to visit emigrant ships lying in the river and needed a shore headquarters. He and members of his congregation took over a closed public house, the *Spread Eagle,* and converted it into a rest and recreation centre, providing educational opportunities and services. General Gordon, who died at Khartoum in 1885, was one of the workers.

The Rev. C. E. Robinson wrote a letter to a leading church journal in 1868 suggesting that anyone who had lost a loved one should help to build a mission hall instead of a costly marble memorial. Miss Beaufort, daughter of Admiral Sir Francis Beaufort, replied, and promised to meet the cost of erection if the foundations were built up to the level of the road. This challenge was met by willing workers, and the foundation stone was laid on St. Peter's Day, 1870, the church being consecrated on St. Andrew's Day, 1871, 'To the Glory of God and in memory of Admiral Sir Francis Beaufort, K.C.B.'.

The interior of the roof of pitch pine is like the inside of an upturned boat, with the beams as thwarts, and the mosaic above the altar depicts 'The Stilling of the Tempest'. The windows also depict religious subjects.

In order to find space for the church on the quay, part of the old public house was pulled down, the remaining portion being known as the Mission House.

The church was closed in 1970 and has now been acquired by the Corporation for an arts centre.

Just beyond the church there is an attractive view of the river across a pleasant riverside lawn, the property of the owners of the *Clarendon Royal* hotel, which dominates the southern side of the road. The title of 'Royal' and of 'Clarendon' have full justification in history, part of the hotel standing upon the site of the residence built for James II when, as Duke of York, he was appointed High Admiral. As he married Anne, daughter of Edward, Earl of Clarendon, the selection of the name of his spouse was a natural one.

The extreme west end of the *Clarendon,* formerly the *Clarendon Shades,* was for some years until 1952 in the occupation of a Mr. Combers, who rejoiced in the literary appellation of Captain Silver. Here he accumulated a large and varied collection of ship's models and nautical gear, fitting up the upper floor overlooking the river as a steam-ship's bridge. A small riding-light hung over the doorway, doorway, and adjacent to the *Clarendon* lawns anchors of vessels that have long passed into the breaker's yards found a resting-place. The whole collection of models is

13.—Entrance porch *Clarendon*, *c.* 1800

now in the National Maritime Museum at Greenwich, the figureheads being in the *Cutty Sark*.

At the rear of the *Clarendon*, set back from the Terrace, was a long building known as 'Clarendon Cottage'. It was once known as 'Grape Vine Cottage', and in the last quarter of the 18th century was the Milton parish workhouse. Nearby on the north side of the Terrace was a large double-fronted house demolished about 1950, which was the last common lodging house in the town. In the 19th century it was the residence of the Pinching's, who for three generations were doctors in the town (see New Road, Chapter Eight).

The area now occupied by houses and boat-repairing yard was occupied by the Terrace Gardens (which extended from the rear of the *Clarendon* hotel under the north-south Royal Pier Road as far as the War Department property and from the river to the Terrace) and was laid out in 1833. Pleasantly landscape-gardened, with flower beds and shrubs and winding walks, it was the rendezvous both of residents and visitors who obtained admission by ticket or payment at toll-offices, which were situated on each side of the Harmer Street entrance on the north side of the Terrace. They were, after being semi-derelict for a number of years, closed, and houses built in the early years of this century.

The pier, designed by J. B. Redman, is now the headquarters of the Trinity House pilots. In Gravesend's palmy days it was a busy landing and embarkation point for visitors brought by paddle-steamer in thousands in the summer season. A temporary pier was first erected in 1835 slightly to the west of the present pier, which was opened in 1842. It was from this pier that the Princess Royal of England, daughter of Queen Victoria, left the shores of England on 2 January 1858 as the bride of Prince William of Prussia. It was bitterly cold and snowed all day. Here, too, in 1863, Princess Alexandra of Denmark first set foot on English soil when she came to this country to wed Edward, Prince of Wales, later King Edward VII. In 1874 the Duke and Duchess of Edinburgh landed here after their marriage. The Duchess was the only daughter of Tsar Alexander II of Russia. The Duke was Earl of Kent and Later Duke of

Saxe-Coburg Gotha. The pier was on occasions the place of departure of Queen Victoria when she made her voyages to the Continent in the earlier part of her reign.

Harmer Street, built in 1836, was part of a design by Amon Henry Wilds for the Milton Park Estate Company. It was originally intended to have a second crescent opposite Berkley Crescent with a road (now The Grove, but then called Upper Harmer Street) leading to Windmill Hill. Only the northern part of the scheme consisting of Berkley Crescent and Harmer Street was carried out. This road is now a conservation area and still has an air of faded dignity. Harmer Street owes its name to the fact that James Harmer, an alderman of the City of London, who resided at Ingress Abbey, Greenhithe, played an important part in the development of the scheme, both financially and administratively.

In 1887 the clock tower was erected to commemorate the Golden Jubilee of Queen Victoria. The total cost was £1,097 –£756 19s. for the tower, £66 17s. 6d. for the architect, £225 for the clock, and £48 for sundries. The architect was John Johnson, who was also responsible for some of the buildings in The Grove, including the butcher's shop at the junction with Parrock Street. The foundation stone was laid on 10 September 1887, and was completed on 9 November 1889, although the chimes presented by Alfred Tolhurst were not completed until February 1890. It is usually stated that the clock and chimes came from the London Road tower at Rosherville Gardens, and certainly the clock was removed from the tower at about this time, but no mention of this appears in the contemporary reports in the papers which give the clockmakers as Smith and Son of Derby, and the bells cast by Warner and Co. of Cripplegate. There were previously shrubs enclosed within artistic iron railings on the north side of Milton Road, filling in the arcs of the Crescent. The last of the acacia trees round Berkley Crescent survived until 1968, and the colonnade was complete until about 1920.

At the north end of Harmer Street on its eastern side there stood until 1955 a stucco-covered building with an ionic portico which had been built in 1836 as The Literary Institution. It originally contained a reading room and lending

14.—Literary Institution, *c.* 1835

library, a lounge and promenade, a billiards room and an assembly room for concerts, recitals, lectures and balls: furnished with a very fine organ it was much patronised by visitors to the town until the 1840s–1850s. It was also known as 'The Assembly Rooms'. As the fortunes of Gravesend as a holiday centre decreased, its fortunes, too, diminished, and for some seasons it was known as 'Kelner's Bazaar' after its proprietor. In the 1890s an extensive reconstruction took place: the broad gallery which stretched along its northern side was taken down, galleries at the west end constructed, and the building reorientated to conform to the required shape of a theatre, becoming first *The Prince of Wales Theatre of Varieties* and later still *The Grand Theatre of Varieties.* The coming of cinema to the town from 1910 onwards introduced competition which the *Grand* was unable to stand against, and it closed in 1933, although the bar remained open. In 1952 the roof fell in, and in 1955 it was rebuilt as a public-house, and because of its former function, was given the name of *The Call-Boy.*

Chapter Ten

MILTON ROAD

THE END of the previous chapter brought us to the Jubilee clock tower, a turn to the right leads after about 100 yards to the cross roads of Parrock Street, Queen Street, King Street, and Milton Road, the point from which the previous chapter started. It is worth noting that the west-east road from the Northfleet boundary (Chapter Seven) has changed its name four times in not much more than a half-mile. From London Road it has become Overcliffe, New Road, King Street, and now is Milton Road, and a mile farther east is Rochester Road.

In 1830 it was possible to stand at the junction of Milton Road–Parrock Street and look in a south-easterly direction over open fields to Milton church and the higher ground towards Cobham. The streets that now occupy the triangle formed by Parrock Street, Wellington Street and Milton Road will be dealt with in a later chapter.

On the left hand, at the corner of Queen Street is the *New* inn, a house with several interesting associations. Originally the place of residence of Lord Paston, it became later the property of Dr. Holker, who in April 1734, entertained there the Prince and Princess of Orange, the latter the daughter of George II, when they were weather-bound on their return to Holland after their marriage.

The property being available for purchase in 1780 when the *New Tavern* (Chapter Eleven) had to be vacated on its requisition by the War department for construction of waterside defences, the licensee, named Ward, removed to Dr. Holker's house, for which he obtained a licence, and gave it the title of the *New inn*. At that time the grounds attached to the house were extensive, reaching nearly as far as the western side of where Harmer Street is now, and covering the area upon which Berkley Road, Wilfred Street and Bernard Street were built in the 1880s. Part of this ground was made into a bowling green, and thus the *New Tavern* green habitués were able to indulge in their favourite pastime in fresh surroundings. From the former bowling green was brought a memorial stone to one of the former bowlers, Alderman Nynn of the Gravesend Corporation, upon which was inscribed a verse extolling his skill at bowls. In the 19th century this was removed to the bowling green of the *Prince of Wales* inn, near Milton church. When the road through Gravesend in the early years of the 19th century allowed stage-coaches to pass along this main street of Gravesend, the *New inn* became one of the halts for such vehicles. The building included the present shops adjoining the *New inn*, the extent of which can be clearly seen from the roof-line.

The church on the south side of the road at the corner of Parrock Street has a curious history, although it is little more than a century old. In the 1830s, when the population of Gravesend and Milton had become double that of 30 years previous (9,445 against 4,539) and the town was a holiday resort as well as a residential and business district, the two parish churches of Gravesend and Milton were unable to accommodate the Church of England worshippers of that time, and a scheme to build a 'proprietary chapel' by a group of local residents and businessmen was launched, a company being formed having a capital of £5,000 in £50 shares. The church was built in 1834, the architect being a Mr. Jenkins. It cost £7,200, which greatly exceeded the estimate of £3,950, and the shares declined in value, being advertised within a year at a 20 per cent. reduction.

The church was put up for auction at the London Auction Mart on 21 July 1842, but although the particulars stated that 'the purchaser was not restrained as to use' and that 'a residence or several houses might be built on the ornamental gardens which surrounded it' no purchaser was found. In 1843 it was bought for £4,000 by the Rev. W. J. Blew, curate of St. Anne's, Westminster. Previously it had been offered to the Rochester diocesan authorities, but the Archdeacon of Rochester was only prepared to pay £3,500.

The Rev. Blew ministered here until 1851, the year of the so-called 'Papal Aggression' (when the Roman Catholic

Church established their Hierarchy in this country) when he and other High Church members of the Church of England wrote to Cardinal Wiseman regretting the way he had been received in England. This lead to a complaint to the Bishop of Rochester, who inhibited the Rev. Blew from performing service for six months. In July 1851 Mr. Blew sold the church to Cardinal Wiseman for £4,000, the Raphael family of Parrock Manor contributing a large part of the purchase price, and the chapel became a Roman Catholic church. A new steeple with saddleback roof was added to the church in 1873 by Goldie and Child, and adjoining premises secured as a convent and school run by the Sisters of Mercy. In 1955 the convent was removed to more extensive premises at Hillside in Old Road East. Alongside the church an organisation called the Mechanics Institute had its library and lecture-room in the early 19th century, but this failed for lack of support.

The next building calling for notice in this road is the handsome Methodist church (architect Derek Buckler and Partners) on the north side of the road, which was erected in 1906 on the site of the first Wesleyan chapel, whose foundation stone was laid in 1819 by the Rev. Joseph Benson, a close friend of John Wesley, whose evangelistic zeal led to the world-wide extension of the Methodist movement. The old building was very plain of structure, but in 1841 it was enlarged and a new front designed, having arched windows and a pediment above in the classical style, within which the words 'Wesleyan Chapel' were incised. Iron railings enclosed a narrow space in which bodies of deceased members of the church were interred.

Opportunity was taken both in 1906 and 1956 to extend the site and provide space for the many activities connected with the church. Here were held the concerts of the Pleasant Sunday Afternoon Association, usually known as the P.S.A., and later the Gravesend Philharmonic Society gave choral concerts here.

Crossing to the south side of the road and viewing the clock tower and Berkley Crescent as one, it is possible to visualise from the colonnade of the shop on the western side of Harmer Street what the Crescent must have been like when it had a colonnade along its whole length, with a covered footway and above a balcony for residents to occupy in sunny weather.

The post office, on the corner of The Grove since 1869, has occupied premises in Milton since 1842. Previously it was in New Road for a few years after its removal from Church Street (Chapter Five). With the expansion of post office functions and payment of pensions, it has outgrown the premises of the 1890s, ousted the postmaster from his apartments and absorbed a dwelling-house in The Grove. The conveyance of letters and parcels now performed mainly by rail had one lingering connection with pre-rail days when, in the closing years of the 19th century a four-horse coach drew up just before midnight at the post office from Rochester, unloaded bags of mail, and loaded others before departing for Dartford, where horses were changed and the coach proceeded to London, the London coach returning to Rochester with its load drawn by the changed horses. This coach service was the result of a dispute between the post office and the railways when the former began to carry parcels, and to protect their own parcel services the railways charged the post office a high price for this traffic. In 1887 the post office started running coaches to Brighton, and a number of other services followed, including one to Chatham which served Gravesend. The last of these coaches finished running in 1909.

Separated from the post office by a private house there was at the same period a wheelwright's yard and shop. Here iron tyres were shrunk on to wooden cart wheels by placing the red-hot tyre around the wheel and binding it on by applications of a quantity of cold water poured from spouted cans. Adjoining this yard at a slightly earlier date was a corn, hay and straw dealer, in the day when feed and bedding for horses were essentials as important as the petrol supply of the present day.

On the opposite side of the road between the *British Tar* and the *Globe* was a row of shops, intersected by Bentley Street. No. 25, now only a one-storey building, was before 1894 a grocer's shop, kept by George Newman, who also aspired to poetry, he having had conferred upon him the bardic title of Lloegryn.

Adjoining Love Lane, the narrow pathway at the back of Wellington Street, where now is a row of shops and yard belonging to the Co-operative, there was in the years between the two world wars a large timber yard which was engulfed in a huge fire in 1928. Before that time there stood on the site Cumberland House, a day and boarding school for boys, kept by James Mallinson, who had removed the school from Park House opposite in 1893. Cumberland Avenue was built in 1899, but Cumberland Terrace, the row of tall buildings farther east, dates back to the very early years of the 19th century, and was in 1830 the only building on the south side of Milton Road. Just beyond is the Milton Road entrance to the former barracks. Within this roadway, just outside the barrack gates was a small conventicle of a group of Baptists. In 1962 when Trinity schools were burnt down the school was moved to a site just inside this entrance to the barracks and it is now to be rebuilt on the barracks site.

Park Place, which occupied the north side of Milton Road, at this point, was in the 19th century an impressive row of semi-detached houses with stucco fronts by Amon Henry Wilds, with its own accommodation road behind a park-fenced shrubbery. With a clear view of the Thames and its shipping at the rear of the houses, it was a popular place of residence by the gentry of the town. It also attracted a number of proprietors of private schools, one of which, Park House, later occupied as an office of the Associated Portland Cement Co., Ltd., and later still as the head-quarters of the Gravesend Conservative party, is mentioned in a preceding paragraph. The houses were pulled down at the end of 1957 and flats built on part of the site. The remaining part was used for the new telephone exchange. One house at the extreme east end of Park Place survived until 1971, but this has now gone.

It will be noted that Milton Road a little farther on veers to the right over a railway bridge before turning back in the former direction towards Milton church, seen about 200 yards beyond. This deviation was made in the late 1860s. Before this time the road continued along what is now Prospect Grove to a level crossing, the old crossing-keeper's cottage having recently been pulled down. There was also a halt here known as Milton Road between 1906 and 1915. On the right-hand side of the present road on the brow of the hill is a building largely of corrugated iron used as a recruiting centre and drill hall. This building formerly stood in Wrotham Road near the junction with Essex Road, where it was *The Pavilion,* a theatre of Gravesend's holiday resort days. The very pleasantly-laid-out gardens bordering the road next to it are a great improvement upon the ugly advertisement hoardings which formerly occupied the site. The Imperial Paper mills bowling green with its clubhouse set off the aspect. A pleasant row of mock Georgian houses have recently been built on the north side of the road, screening the railway.

Although not in Milton Road with which this chapter deals, the Gravesend School for Boys (formerly the Grammar school, and prior to 1944 the County school) comes more conveniently under this heading than under any other. It lies behind the garden of Milton rectory, opposite the church on the south side of Milton Road, and access is reached from Church Walk, which leads southward on the Gravesend side of the rectory.

The school is a modern building, the first block, then known as 'the workshop block' being erected in 1931. The land had been acquired from Bernard Arnold, the son of George Matthews Arnold, in 1924, for use as a playing field for the Junior Technical school in Darnley Road, out of which the present school developed (see Chapter Thirteen). A pavilion was erected on the playing field and between 1931 and 1938 work proceeded on additional buildings, the school moving in to the new buildings in the latter year. The official opening took place on 12 October 1938, the then chairman of the Kent County Council, Edward Hardy, Esq., performing the opening ceremony.

Seventeen classrooms are provided, an assembly hall, with stage (upon which school plays are presented at regular intervals), laboratories and workshops, headmaster's and staff rooms, offices, etc. There are also hutments to provide room for activities for which convenient rooms in the main building are not available. Extensive playing fields stretch eastwards towards Denton. A heated swimming bath also has been recently added.

At the top of the hill, now the 480 'bus terminus, and once the terminus of the Gravesend tramway is the eastern limit of Milton parish, which was for many years the boundary of the borough of Gravesend and the limit of the built-up areas. Beyond are Denton and Chalk, formerly separated from the municipal area, but included within the borough from 1935. This portion of the Gravesend administrative district will be surveyed in a later chapter.

15.—Milton church, *c.* 1790

Milton church, dedicated to St. Peter and St. Paul, approached from the west by a long flagstone pathway, dates back to the 14th century, but earlier than this a church stood in Milton, at least from Saxon times. What antiquarians regard as a surviving remnant of an earlier church on this site is to be seen low down at the south-west corner, where a filled-in arch is part of the present structure: but this cannot confidently be regarded as part of the church existing here in 1086 and noted in Domesday Book.

If, instead of entering by the war memorial lych-gate at the west end of the paved pathway we walk a few yards up the hill, a wrought iron gate of handsome design, bearing a replica of Gravesend's first coat of arms of date 1568 is seen at a point where the churchyard wall is observed to be of different construction than that farther westward. The reason for the difference is that until the early 19th century the churchyard terminated here. In 1805 a piece of manorial waste ground was taken into the churchyard, and in the following year some more land was added on the north side. Both the lych-gate and the iron gate were erected in 1951.

As we enter by this gateway, the sundial over what was from the 16th century onward until 1819 the south porch of the church claims notice with its motto, 'Trifle not, your time's but short'. This remarkable sundial deserves close attention for its many interesting features. It has recently been restored by the rector, the Rev. Hilary Day. It was designed by James Giles, master of the Free school in King Street (noticed in Chapter Eight), and bears witness to his scientific knowledge and attainments. The porch was used as a vestry for many years and is now a small chapel or shrine.

The tower, under which we enter through the west doorway, is probably a little later date than the body of the church. It contains a peal of eight bells and is topped by a crown and Prince of Wales's feathers. When this vane was restored in 1954 by Mr. W. G. Harpum a strip of metal inside had the words 'G. Thomas 1842' on it, and Mr. Harpum added his own name and the date. There is a story that when the work was being done in 1842 Queen Victoria passed in her carriage with the infant Prince of Wales en route for London, and hearing the bells being tolled in her honour authorised the addition of the Prince of Wales feathers. Five of the bells were hung in 1656, one in 1810, and the other two in 1930. The clock was added in 1875.

The base of the tower acts as porch and in the left corner is the stairway to the ringing chamber and the belfry, whilst the doorway ahead leads into the rather narrow interior, there being no side aisles, with a gallery on the north side and a west gallery largely occupied by the organ. This was

16.—Milton church, schools and rectory, *c.* 1865

installed in 1829 as a barrel organ, was rebuilt in 1887, and renovated in 1936. A door on the left, formerly the north door, leads to the vestries, built and furnished in 1950. The interior is an interesting example of 18th-century plastering and ceiling and dates from 1790 when the old lead roof was removed, the walls were increased by two feet, and the present slated roof put on. The work was done by Thos. Hall of Dartford, and the addition to the walls can clearly be traced on the outside.

There is no physical chancel, but there is a sedila on the south side under the south-east window. The corbels of a previous roof still exist, with grotesque heads and other carving. On the eastern wall of the church is to be seen the outline of what was either a very large window or, as has been suggested, a former chancel arch.

It only remains now in this chapter to note the rectory on the south side of the road, built in 1860, and the *Prince of Wales* public house, which, at the end of the 18th century, was a farmhouse. The field to the north of the church, where Raphael Road and the railway now lie, was called Miller's field, and it is probable that the mill mentioned in the Domesday Survey was a tide-mill near here. The river would have flowed up to this area before the river walls were built, and the marshes drained. It was for this mill that William Morton paid 19½ pence rent in 1393, and from which 'Milton' probably obtained its name.

Milton Road Primary School was opened on 18 October 1884 by the Mayor, George Hubert Edmonds and closed at the end of the Summer term 1976. Milton Church School opened in 1860 and closed in 1938 is now used as the Parish Hall. It was always known as "The Duck Pond School" from the pond which adjoined the site to the North.

Chapter Eleven

MILTON PLACE, WHITEHALL PLACE AND TRINITY CHURCH

WE HAVE NOW COVERED the whole of that part of Gravesend north of the main road, with the exception of that portion lying east of Harmer Street. A convenient starting-point for this section is the junction of Milton Place and Ordnance Road with Milton Road. In the angle of these two roads until 1963 stood Holy Trinity church, a cruciform building in the decorated style with a tower forming the porch at the south-west end of the nave. The architect was J. Wilson, and the church, built of Kentish rag and slated, had a series of carved heads round the cornice, and an elaborate hammer-beam roof. It was originally intended to have a spire, but this was never built, and the tower was finished with an open-work parapet and four pinnacles at the corners. It cost £4,300 to build and received a grant of £600 under the Church Building Act. When built in 1844 it seated 1,000.

The scheme for the erection of a new church had the approval of the diocesan authorities after the archdeacon's failure to purchase St. John's. The site for Holy Trinity was given by the Board of Ordnance, who owned the land northwards to the river on condition that seats were made available for customs officers. The corner-stone was laid in May 1844 by the then Countess of Darnley. The consecration took place on 21 August 1845, and the first incumbent was the Rev. Richard Joynes.

The church became within a very short time the 'fashionable' church in the town. The provision of a very fine organ fostered the musical side of the services, and the congregation included a large proportion of the more prosperous waterside community—pilots, customs officers, and watermen, with their families. The congregation, however, dwindled as the residential area moved to the south of the town after the 1939–45 war. The ragstone deteriorated very badly, and although some work of restoration was done and a new east window inserted, the church became unsafe and was demolished in 1963. It was here that the Trinity Sunday Pilots' Service was first held in 1908, a senior representative of Trinity House (the governing body of the pilot service) usually attending. When the church was demolished in 1963 the service was transferred to St. George's, where it continues to attract a large congregation.

A project for building a school adjacent to the church was launched in 1865 and a building in ragstone with decorated Gothic windows was erected. This building was destroyed by fire in 1962, when the school was moved to Milton barracks.

Milton Place, the road leading directly north to the riverside, was when it was first built in the early years of the 19th century a very desirable place of residence as it commanded a prospect over meadows to the lower part of Gravesend Reach and the Lower Hope in which could be seen, either at anchor or under sail, the great three-masters bringing overseas produce from the Far East and the southern seas. Here, too, at No. 10, was the double-fronted Penny's Library, established in 1826, where visitors and residents foregathered to exchange gossip and indulge in leisurely reading. A memory of this period was enshrined in the name Library Place, a turning on the left which led to Bentley Street.

Opposite the point where East Terrace joins Milton Place are the handsome gates of Fort Gardens. These lead into New Tavern Fort, built in 1779/80, and now laid out as public gardens. The fort was re-modelled in 1868–72 to take 10 heavy guns, mostly 9-inch 12-ton rifled muzzle loaders. Some of the emplacements for these guns still exist and the magazines underneath are virtually intact with their special arrangements for lighting. In 1905 two 6-inch converted breech-loading guns were installed in separate emplacements overlooking the promenade. There is a separate magazine for these two guns which survives complete with shell and cartridge hoists. It was garrisoned until the end of the First World War. The commander during that period was a Major Crookshank, who carried out a historical survey of the Chantry. In 1930 the Corporation acquired the site from the Government (having previously bought the moat and land adjoining the promenade in 1910) and laid out the gardens which were opened in 1932 by the Earl of Darnley as part of the celebration of the Mayoral Tercentenary. The beauty and arrangement of these gardens are striking testimony to the aim of successive councillors and aldermen of the borough to provide both for residents and visitors a restful recreational centre sheltered on the north and east from chill winds, and in which concerts and other entertainments are held. An earlier generation only knew of this areas as a mysterious enclosure behind unclimbable walls and embankments with a formidable spiked iron railing protecting a moat. Stores and married quarters of a detachment of Royal Engineers occupied buildings fronting the site. Abutting upon the roadway a little farther south stood Fort House, the residence of the Commanding Royal Engineer, who from 1869 to 1871 was General Gordon, known as 'Chinese Gordon', who met his death at at Khartoum in 1885. In the 1830s it was a private school and later a private dwelling-house, at one time the residence of the town clerk.

It was in Fort House that Gordon entertained the lads from the poorer parts of Gravesend, seeing that they were well fed on their visits, teaching them the rudiments of reading and writing and arithmetic at a time when there were very few facilities for education, giving them instruction in Christian belief and behaviour, and finding the most worthy of them employment. His interest in their physical well-being and growth was evidenced for many years after his death by a scale in feet and inches scored upon one of the door frames which was used to measure the growth in height of boys from the time of their first becoming his 'kings' for entry in a logbook kept for that purpose. Opportunities for recreation were provided by permission to play cricket and other games in the 'Captain's Field', now part of the recreation ground adjoining the promenade.

Unfortunately, Fort House was reduced to a heap of ruins by the explosion of the warhead of one of the

17.—Gravesend, by J. Lock. Chantry blockhouse with bridge and St. Georges Tower, 1812

V2 rocket missiles reaching Gravesend during the 1939–45 war. (This projectile, or what remained of it, could be seen for many years afterwards within the fort grounds.) This event took place in 1944. It also demolished houses on the west side of Milton Place, together with the former Milton tithe barn which had for many years been leased by the Corporation as a yard where the dust carts were kept. During the 1939–45 war Fort House was used as the food office. The site of Fort House is now a rose garden, with bricks marking the foundations.

Just before reaching the promenade on the right is Milton chantry, Gravesend's earliest existing building, still with its original roof timbers of the late 13th century. This chantry chapel was re-founded about 1321 by Aymer de Valence, Earl of Pembroke, on the site of a hospital founded in 1189. An outline of its history is given at the end of this chapter.

The roadway at this point comes to an end with only a footway to the Gordon promenade to the right: this will be considered later. Straight ahead lies the causeway known as the New Bridge, built upon piles which terminate in a wooden staircase at low tide point. It is impossible not to feel that there is here a great deal of history of which no record remains. When Aymer de Valence endowed the chantry in the 14th century, certain lands in Essex were charged with its support. These were in Nevendon, Vange and South Benfleet, and it is reasonable to suppose that contributions in kind were brought across the river to be landed at a spot near to the chantry, rather than landing them at the Town Quay to be brought down over rough roads and paths to their destination. If so, it is possible that a landing-place existed here six centuries ago, and that this became in time a public landing-place. In the early 19th century the causeway and bridge were repairable by the Vestry of Milton, items such as, 'to planking and repairing rails on causeway, New Tavern, 16s' (1809), and in the

18.–Chantry interior, showing roof constructions, Borough arms, 1562, left, 1632 right

same year, 'drawing 45 feet of plank round the causeway, £1.2.6'; entries that suggest that the parish was responsible for the upkeep of a public way to the river.

Later, it became known as Wates's Bridge, the hotel upon its western side being kept by a licensee of that name. It was a hotel at which Charles Dickens occasionally resided: it became known later as the *Commercial* hotel. It had an outlet from its riverside to the New Bridge as well as possessing a quay of its own. In the early years following the first World War it was taken over by the Sea School authorities, the old building was demolished and the Sea School itself extended to provide facilities for training of youth for the Merchant Navy.

The main Sea School building on the landward side was, from 1886 onwards until its acquisition for youth training purposes in 1918, the Sailor's Home, where sailors of all nations could procure lodgings between discharge from one voyage to signing-on for another. The Sea School was moved to new premises on Denton Marshes in 1967 and the building was demolished in 1975.

Outside the main gates of the Sea School was the garage of the St. John Ambulance Association, and near by up a short flight of steps an office occupied in the late 19th century as a Royal Engineers' office.

The large Customs House which adjoins was erected in 1816 to house the Excise authorities on a site formerly occupied by the *Fountain* inn, which was transferred to the south side of the highway and remained there until 1914. In 1836 the Board of Customs removed from its earlier offices in Whitehall Place, as the line of houses between Milton Place and East Terrace is named, into the Excise building, with direct access to the river. The end house in Whitehall Place from which the Board removed was destroyed as a result of the enemy action mentioned earlier in this chapter. It had a-top a look-out with glass front from which vessels coming up the river might be seen at a great distance. Offices in Whitehall Place, now occupied by commercial firms, were until just before the Second World War in the occupation of other waterside authorities. In one of the houses Robert Pierce Cruden, author of *A History of Gravesend(*(1843), resided for a time.

With the *Terrace* hotel, the Terrace proper begins, the roadway on the left, probably following a very old footway, being known as East Terrace. The Terrace was built in 1791 by James Leigh Joynes, the first row of houses to be constructed in the town as a private venture. He also paved the footway at his own expense. The ground upon which the southern side of the Terrace was built was known in the 17th century as 'The Camps'. It was also known as the Sconce lands, a sconce being a small fort. Pocock records the existence of earthworks here and that the debris resulting from the disastrous fire of 1727 (Chapter Three) was used to level this area. This thoroughfare issues at its western end into Queen Street (Chapter Nine).

Having now covered the whole of the area east of Harmer Street we may now return to a brief history of the chantry. From the 14th century onwards there seem to have been difficulties, partly due to the insufficiency of the endowment provided, and the advowson of Milton church was added to the chantry which was 'in honour of the Virgin Mary and the Apostles Peter and Paul', which latter saints, it will be noted, are those whose names are borne by Milton church. The chantry priests celebrated offices in Milton church and some of them were rectors of Milton.

A number of disputes between the diocesan authorities and the patrons of the chantry occurred from time to time, and the building suffered decay. In 1524 Sir Thomas Wyatt was given a licence to found a chantry in the old chapel of St. Mary in Milton, but it is doubtful if this was ever done. It was eventually let to William Wylde of Milton, when the property, now lost to ecclesiastical purposes, was described as 'all that chapel in Melton, called Melton Chapel, together with the hall, pantry, kitchen, storehouse, chambers, &c. with their appurtenances belonging to it, and also one wharf, one orchard, a pond, two gardens, and two closes of land lying on the south and east sides of the said chapel, containing 13 acres. . . '. Pocock adds to the above quoted description that all that remained of it in 1778 was the chapel part of which was built chiefly of flints and rag stones, and that it was cased over with brick in 1781. This brick casing has been since removed in places to reveal some of the flint construction.

In 1697, the chantry had become an alehouse, and it remained so, its title being changed from the *Zoar* alehouse to the *New Tavern* in the following century. It so remained until 1781, when the Board of Ordnance acquired the property and demolished 10 houses on the northern side in preparation for the erecting of the bastions of the fort. As stated in Chapter Ten the landlord of the *New Tavern* removed to Dr. Holker's house in Milton Road, which he named the *New inn.*

A newspaper of 1846 records that whilst digging foundations for a magazine many skeletons of former occupants were found.

The existing buiding which is of flint, ragstone and rubble construction, with some of the interior lined with chalk blocks, seems to have been the cross wing of a timber-framed building which abutted on its south side. This building, together with the chantry was encased in bricks at the end of the 18th century, and, after being used at one time as the residence of the rector of Milton, became a row of cottages which were demolished in 1969. In 1972, after protracted negotiations, the Ministry of the Environment agreed to restore the chantry with the assistance of grants from the Pilgrim Trust and other bodies, and to take the building into guardianship. It is of interest to note that from 1938 until 1945 it was used as a centre for Air Raid Precautions, and fitted up with showers for gas decontamination. In the First World War troops used it as barracks. More recently it has been used by the Borough band, the Scouts, and as a local museum, maintained by the Gravesend Historical Society.

Chapter Twelve

THE PROMENADE AND CANAL AREA

FROM THE ROADWAY at the head of the New Bridge where our last chapter closed, a turn to the right leads to the Gordon Promenade. The promenade is of comparatively recent construction and until the late 1880s was largely a stretch of saltings covered at high spring tide nearly up to the wall surrounding the fort, and at other times a repository of seaweed and flotsam of all kinds. Advantage was taken of the sinking of a schooner loaded with bags of cement to purchase the damaged cargo and erect with them an embankment, the ground behind being levelled to the required height. Some of the built-up cement bags are still evidenced by the pattern of the fabric on the firmly-set blocks. A bandstand was built in 1890 at a cost of £100 and further land was bought from the railway in 1902, and in 1906 shelters were built.

Just on the left as the promenade is entered from what was once known as Commercial Place are the boat-sheds and clubhouse of Gravesend Rowing Club, established in 1878.

For many years there stood at a point near the north-west corner of the present canal basin what was known as the Round Tree. This was regarded as marking the seaward limit of the Port of London, beyond which the duty on coal entering the port was not chargeable. This was a convenient, rather than an exact landmark, as the eastward end of the parish of Milton is some distance farther east. The tree was damaged by gun practice from the fort towards the end of the 18th century, and early in the 19th century was mischievously set on fire, sailors from a collier lying in the Canal Basin extinguishing the flames. Its end came by being blown down during a violent storm, with strong winds from the south-south-west on the night of 5 August 1825.

After the destruction of the tree, an obelisk was set up in its place in 1826 and when excavations were made for its foundation bricks were found similar to those used in the Gravesend blockhouse, from which it would seem that this was the site of the Milton blockhouse. Excavation on the spot by a small group of the Gravesend Historical Society in February 1973 has confirmed the existence of these foundations. From early maps earthworks are known to have existed here. The use of this stone as a landmark being no longer needed, it was taken down and lay for many years on the edge of the Canal Basin. In 1892 it was re-erected at the entrance to the Gordon Memorial Gardens, but with no mention of its former function.

The playing ground on the south side of the promenade was part of the fort grounds until late in the 19th century, being known as 'The Captain's Field'. It was in 1886 that it was leased to the Corporation and became the first public recreation field, with the familiar name of 'The Rec', and was purchased in 1910. Here, in 1911, Gravesend's first municipal swimming bath was built, to be filled in when the larger swimming bath in Ordnance Road was opened in 1938. The ornamental water on the western side of this ground was originally the moat surrounding the fort, and together with the Glen was laid out in 1911.

Adjoining 'The Captain's Field' on the east are the Gordon Memorial Gardens, the ground itself and their original lay-out being due to the munificence in 1890 and 1892 of George Mathews Arnold, J.P., eight times mayor of Gravesend. A metal plate on the plinth of the before-mentioned obelisk records the circumstances of the gift of the gardens and the eastern part of the foreshore.

Across Ordnance Road, or, as it was earlier known, Coal Road (because much of the coal landed in the Canal Basin was transported along this road to the town), the large red brick building is the Gordon Secondary School, completed in 1932. The triangular ground upon which it is placed was formerly a grass field affording pasture for cows, kept by a dairyman of Queen Street, 'Joble' King. Until the 1920s he or his sons used to drive these cows up Milton Road and down Queen Street to be milked each day at his dairy. At other times it was used as a football field. Opposite are the municipal swimming baths mentioned earlier in this chapter.

The road in front of the Gordon School forks to become Albion Terrace on the right branch (later Norfolk Road). The first three turnings, Albion, Augustine, and Brunswick Roads, were built upon what was known in the 18th century as East India Field, the chartered company of that name using it as a site for a camp for its soldiers when their ships were moored in the river off Gravesend. The three roads form thoroughfares to Milton Road, as do Prospect Place and St. John's Road farther on. Much of this area was cleared for re-development in 1972. On the corner of Norfolk Road and St. John's Road is one of the earliest pillar boxes in the country, dating from 1855.

By taking the left fork towards the river and skirting the Gordon Memorial Gardens, the Canal Basin is reached, and nearer the riverside the road over the canal entrance which leads to engineering and other works. By the side of the canal entrance is the clubhouse of the Gravesend Sailing Club, founded in 1894, whose members use the Canal Basin for laying up and fitting-out their craft. At the eastern end of the Canal Basin there stood until 1942 a small cottage, the roof of which was an upturned hull of a boat, with a window in one side. This is held by some to have been the inspiration which led Dickens to invent the house of Peggotty in *David Copperfield.* (Peggoty's house, however, is described as being constructed of a vessel in an upright position.) A little farther on there was constructed in the early 1800s the Albion swimming baths, circular in shape, a rival to the Clifton baths at the west end of the riverside (Chapter Four). These failed to succeed as the Clifton baths did, and for many years lay as a muddy pool.

The Thames and Medway Canal, to give it its correct title, was a project which also failed. Its sponsors conceived of it as a means of transporting barges from the Thames to the Medway without the inconvenience and danger of sailing round the Isle of Grain, so saving time and expense. An Act of Parliament was passed in 1800, giving powers to cut the canal across marshland to the high ground at Higham

19.—Boathouse and canal. Denton mill in background, *c.* 1840

and thence by a tunnel two miles in length to the Medway at Strood. The engineer was William Tierney Clark, and it was opened at the Gravesend end on 14 October 1824. The Port of London refused to allow a lock to project into the river, so that it was only possible to leave and enter the canal when the tide was high, which delayed traffic. A steam-boat for passengers to Rochester damaged the banks. Finally in 1845 a single line of railway was laid from a station at the Canal Basin to Strood running through the tunnel on stilts in the water. This was taken over by the North Kent line of the South Eastern Railway in 1849, who filled in the tunnel and doubled the track. The canal continued to be used as far as Higham, where there was a small basin with a wharf until 1935 when it was finally abandoned, and has since been gradually filled up with the exception of the basin which was acquired by the Corporation in 1972 to lay out as a marina and pleasure gardens.

On the south side of the canal stood the former gas and electricity works. The older, formerly the Gravesend and Milton Gas Light and Coke Company's works, were transferred to this part of the town from earlier premises in Bath Street in 1843. The manufacture of gas at Gravesend ceased in 1958, and the works were demolished, only the gas-holders remain. The electricity undertaking was launched in 1900 as a municipal venture, current being first provided for the opening of the electric tramway in August 1902, and for general consumption in 1903. The surplus profits were applied to reduction of the rates. The undertaking was nationalised in 1948 and is under the control of the South Eastern Electricity Board. For some years the station continued to act as an auxiliary station for the national grid, but was finally closed in 1970 and has since been demolished. The first electric street lighting was provided in 1903 when the Corporation installed 12 arc lights in the main road. The change over from gas followed rapidly in Gravesend, but Northfleet continued to use gas for street lighting until after the Second World War, no doubt due to the fact that the current was supplied by the Gravesend Corporation, who extended their supplies into Northfleet from 1905.

Adjoining the above undertakings there stood in the early years of the 19th century the Gravesend station of the Gravesend and Rochester railway mentioned above. It was on the length of canal between this point and the bridge at Denton that rowing boats could be hired and on which skating took place in the winter.

PART TWO

Chapter Thirteen

BETWEEN NEW ROAD AND OLD ROAD: THE WESTERN SECTION

IT IS PROPOSED in the present section to deal with the district lying between the main road and the other west-east road, Old Road, which runs at a distance of about half-mile—more or less—south of the main road.

A convenient starting-point for this section of the Guide is that part of the old municipal boundary in Old Road West near the top of Victoria Road, Northfleet, where the dividing line between the two parishes runs roughly north and south, and as this line is somewhat difficult to follow without some guidance, a brief note of its course may here be given. Near the top of Victoria Road there is on the north side of the Old Road a passageway which may be followed across Havelock Road and at the back of Mayfield Road, Northfleet, towards the railway line. From here the boundary between Northfleet and Gravesend which was the setting-out point of Chapter Seven, which dealt with Overcliffe, may be seen across excavated ground. Returning then to Old Road at the top of Victoria Road, the pedestrian may trace the boundary southward down Victoria Road—marking a stone in the eastern wall—thence across Pelham Road South, and along a passage on the east side of the *Rose* inn (the first house in Perry Street) as far as and along Napier Road until the boundary crosses into municipal property at Dashwood. The line can be picked up again at the boundary stone in Dashwood Road where, after a triangular venture into Woodlands Park, it proceeds across New House Lane, along the rear of Lane's Avenue, Northfleet, and sharp left to Claphall, Wrotham Road (an old boundary stone stands here) and continues across the golf links to Singlewell Road, where there is another stone in the lane just north-west of Gypsy Corner. (The above is the old Gravesend boundary: the district added to it will come within the next Part.) The 'banks and baulks' of the old boundary can be traced in the fields to the west of Wrotham Road and across the golf links, and there is a ditch marking the boundary in Woodlands Park.

Returning again to the original starting-point in Old Road West—described at the beginning of the second paragraph—we may observe that with the exception of a few older houses on the north side, the houses on both sides of the road are comparatively modern having been built in the years following the 1890s. The ground between Pelham Road South, Old Road, and Victoria Road, upon which many of them stand was originally glebe land, i.e., land belonging to the church, the income of which was dedicated to church purposes. (A road leading out of Pelham Road South has been named Glebe Road in commemoration of this fact.)

Along this same Old Road there rattled during the 18th century the stage-coaches conveying passengers between London and Dover, the name of Dover Road, Northfleet, bearing witness to this traffic. In some documents of the period the road is referred to as the London-Paris road. It ceased to be so regarded when soon after 1801 the newer road through the town was followed by the coaches. (See Chapter Eight.)

Arrived at this junction of Pelham Road with Old Road, a choice has to be made of the road to be followed in embracing the triangular area enclosed within Pelham Road, Darnley Road and Old Road, to which the rest of this chapter is devoted. At these crossroads there may have been a settlement in the Saxon period. The famous Domesday Book in 1086 makes reference to a church as existing in Gravesend, and we are justified in believing that it stood hereabouts, possibly upon the site of the rear of the *White Post* public house, occupied by later churches until the early 16th century.

Additional evidence of the antiquity of this area was discovered in 1838, at a spot between Salisbury Road and

Cecil Road on the south, near where dairy premises are now, of a hoard of 552 coins, mainly Saxon, bearing evidence of having been struck between 814 and 878 A.D., which had lain buried for nearly 1,000 years. These may have belonged to an ecclesiastic who, when a Danish invasion was imminent, buried them, and did not live to retrieve them, as buried with them was a silver cross about two inches each way with its decoration unfinished.

Proceeding along Pelham Road we pass Havelock Road and Granville Road and reach the *White Post* public house. It was here in the back gardens of a row of cottages now called Pelham Terrace, and formerly Whitepost Terrace, that the first parish church of Gravesend, dedicated to St. Mary, stood. It was rebuilt in 1510 after a fire but ceased to be the parish church in 1544, although it seems to have been derelict or in a state of bad repair for some years prior to this date. What the appearance of this church was is not known. William Crafter, a friend of Robert Pocock, Gravesend's first historian, in his inter-leaved copy of Pocock, inserts a sketch made on 26 November 1822, of the churchyard as he conceived it to be from examination of the site, giving a length of 325 feet and a breadth of 100 feet, and marked in heavy lines the few remains of stone foundations existing at that time. Gravestones, including one carved as though covering the grave of an ecclesiastic, and bones of interred persons have also been found on or near this site. The hedge bordering the road, and some of the foundations were grubbed up in the 1820s, the latter being used for road material. A red floor tile with green glaze dug up at this time is now in the local museum. The site was sold for building in 1844 when the *White Post* and cottages at the rear were built. In front was St. Mary's (sometimes called 'Queen Marys') Green.

Pelham Road did not receive its present name until the middle of the 19th century. Up to that time—and afterwards in common speech—the narrow roadway was known as Manor Lane, from the Manor Farm extending along its south-east side, Style's Lane, from the name of the farmer who tilled the ground, and later White Post Lane. At the junction of Pelham Road and Darnley Road was a pond which in 1823 was the subject of threatened litigation between the representatives of the rector of Gravesend and the Vestry, because the latter body had removed soil from the pond. A reference to this pond is to be found also in the burial registers of Northfleet for 1833. For many years the *White Post* inn retained its dwelling-house aspect with a croquet lawn at the side.

The *White Post* was not always a fully licensed house. It became so in 1846 when an extensive fire in High Street necessitated the hurried removal of the licensee of the *Black Horse,* W. King, who successfully applied for the transfer of his licence to the *White Post.*

The name of the *White Post* inn may be attributed to its proximity to the before-mentioned glebe land. A writer in the early years of the 19th century mentioned the glebe land as being distinguished by white posts set along its borders, and it is thus easy to see the transference of these features to provide the newly-built house with a name.

Opposite the inn is the entrance to the Gravesend School for Girls, erected in 1926, and then known as the Girls' County School, and from 1944, the Grammar School. For many years the land upon which it is built was part of a large stretch of pastureland which extended until the early 20th century as far east as the roadway now known as Arthur Street West and out to the Old Road on the south. Part of this was used during its latter period as a sports field before the school was erected, and today the school's playing field extends as far as The Avenue, which will be mentioned later.

The school was officially opened on 20 October 1926 by the Duchess of Atholl, who was at that time Parliamentary Secretary to the Board of Education. The architect was W. H. Robinson.

Proceeding along Pelham Road on the north-western side of flint-built Bycliffes Terrace, where now is a pair of semi-detached villas, a field extended as far back as Campbell Road, where in the early 1890s Gravesend Ormonde football club played. This club was amalgamated with the Gravesend town club to become Gravesend United (see Chapter Seven). After passing Lennox Road the next turning on the left is

Grange Road, just within which until 1943 stood a large drill hall used by the Territorials, and in the 1939/45 war as the headquarters of the Home Guard. It was also available for meetings and dances and fetes. It was built to profit by the roller-skating craze of the turn of the century, and was destroyed by enemy action. Grange Road opens out at its western end into Lennox Road, and behind it on the southern side is a diverted path which was until the 1890s a favourite pathway to Southfleet across fields.

The first houses on the west of Pelham Road were built about 1870. One of these calls for notice, 'Mayfield', which before the erection of the School for Girls was the County School for Girls from 1914 to 1926. 'Mayfield' was built in 1875 as a residence by Mr. I. C. Johnson, claimed as the first developer of Portland cement, who died in 1911 aged 101 years. It was one of the earliest concrete houses.

We have now all but arrived at the junction of Pelham Road with Darnley Road which, until the late 18th century, was a roadway within a field closed by gates at both ends. In 1796 the Vestry ordered the gates to be taken away. The northern gate was a few yards south of the present junction.

At the point where Darnley Road and Pelham Road meet there was in the early 19th century a pond, and behind it the homestead of Manor Farm. This was the farmhouse for the Gravesend Manor Farm which belonged to the Earl of Darnley, and his tenant farmed the land from the Northfleet boundary to Windmill Street at one time. The house was demolished about 1880. The pond was filled in, and the pleasant triangular open garden occupies its site and part of the homestead garden. For many years the site was occupied by large hoardings for billposting.

It will be necessary now to turn in a northward direction, first in order to begin the description of Darnley Road at a point where it makes a junction with New Road (see Chapter Eight). The northern part of Darnley Road was known until the late 19th century as Somerset Street, the shops adjoining the *Somerset Arms* public house being at that time private houses. Barrack Row is so-called from a row of very small dwelling-houses which occupied the site of the shops and the rear of the cinema. These dwellings were for a time the married quarters of army personnel.

Dominating Darnley Road opposite Barrack Row and the railway station is Gravesend Technical College Boys' department. It was built in 1893, the architect Lieut.-Col. C. T. Plunkett, and was at one time the Municipal Day School, and had mixed classes of boys and girls. They sat on separate sides of the class and had their own separate playgrounds, entrances and stairs on each side of the building. It was a punishable offence for any of the boys to speak to any of the girls outside school, even though they were in the same class. Later it was known as the School of Science and Art and had sufficient spare room to house the Gravesend Free Library in two of its rooms. It then became the County School for Higher Education when this was taken over by the Kent C.C. In 1931 part of the school was moved to Milton (see Chapter Ten), and in 1939 it was taken over by the Technical School. The Girls' School had earlier outgrown its allotted space within the school in Pelham Road, described earlier in this chapter.

The demand for increased space for scientific education soon caused the eviction of the art side of the college to premises in Overcliffe, where it still continues to expand. (See Chapter Seven.) In order to cope with this growth of demand for space for the technical and engineering side of the college and for evening classes, new buildings have been erected in Pelham Road.

A statue of Queen Victoria in terra-cotta, presented by G. M. Arnold to the town to commemorate the Diamond Jubilee of Her Late Majesty, stands before the college.

Opposite and approached by Barrack Row (the western end of which is Clive Road) and Rathmore Road is the railway station (formerly Gravesend Central), connecting the town with London on the west and the Kent coast and Maidstone and the Medway towns to the east. The station was opened in 1849, the architect being Samuel Beazley, and until 1971 it had a rather pleasant doric portico, the columns of which have now been boxed in by British Railways in an effort to 'modernise' it. The original North Kent line to London Bridge ran via Woolwich

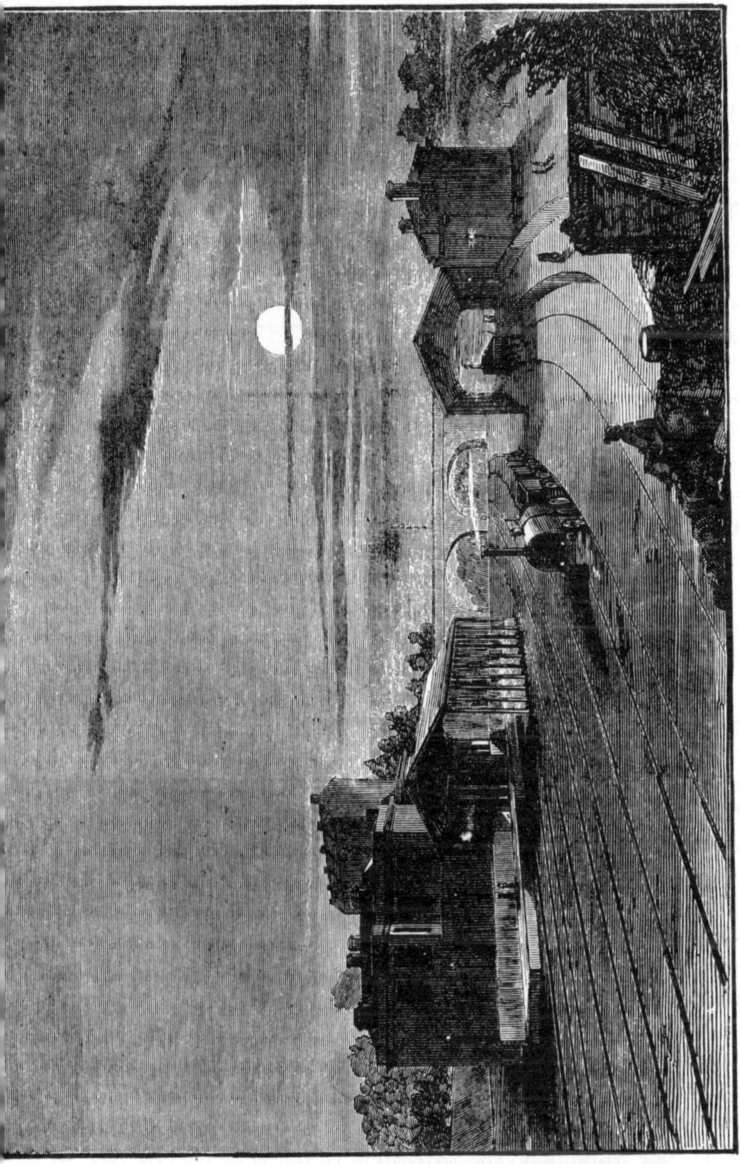

20.—Station, 1849

and Blackheath, and there was one train every two hours, with one extra train up in the morning, and one extra one down at night. After the Dartford loop was built in 1866 most of the London trains ran via Sidcup.

A park for motor cars was constructed by the Corporation in 1957 on land used hitherto as allotment gardens at the rear of Cobham Street, and this is accessible from Rathmore Road, entering upon it from either the Darnley Road or Wrotham Road (Stone Street) ends. The site of the old turntable (removed about 1930) and later bay platform have also become a car park, as has the old goods depot on the down side. The old stable, however, remains now used for car sales.

The streets leading out of Darnley Road on the eastern side, Cobham, Darnley (named out of compliment to the Darnley family), Spencer (from a well-known chemist tradesman), and Arthur Streets, with Trafalgar Road, were built largely between 1840 and 1860, as were other small streets to which they lead–Cutmore and Brandon Streets were so named from owners of the land, Clifton Grove (another Darnley complimentary name) and Nine Elms Grove (stated to be so named because of Nine Elms station in London at a time when it was believed the railway station would be sited in that vicinity). Brandon Street was originally called Station Street when it was intended to build the station at the southern end.

South of Trafalgar Road until the late '90s there was open ground, with the exception of Lynton House (demolished in 1970), which between 1918 and 1926 housed the juniors of the County School for Girls, and was later the Income Tax office. Beside it was a nursery garden with glasshouses. Essex Road and Kent Road belong to the late 'nineties.

At the junction with Old Road a right turn brings us to the corner which we left to explore Pelham Road. On the left, opposite The Avenue, which connects Old Road with Pelham Road, is the sombre front of Gravesend cemetery. It is, perhaps, a grim comment upon Life as a whole to reflect that this was the entrance gate to scenes of gaiety in the '30s and '40s of the last century when the place was known as Victoria Pleasure Gardens, and visitors to Gravesend attended concerts and balls in what is now the cemetery chapel, partook breakfasts and suppers amid scenes of jollity, and practised archery or played bowls where now stand the headstones of graves. The decline of visitors to Gravesend as a result of competing pleasure resorts by the sea brought about a severe diminution in patronage and the proprietors disposed of the gardens to others who there established the cemetery by Private Act of Parliament in 1838. It was taken over in 1905 by the Gravesend Corporation. Since then the area of the cemetery has been extended on more than one occasion and now reaches out more than double the depth of the earlier site. The entrance lodges and gate with Grecian Doric columns were built *c.* 1840 by Amon Henry Wilds (or possibly by Mr. Geary, the cemetery architect). The cemetery gates have now in part been restored.

The next turning on the left, Cecil Road, leads to Cecil Road Primary School which, when it was built in 1909, was known as Cecil Road Board School, and covered a large range of pupils from infants onward to school leaving age. Prior to the erection of the Gordon School in Ordnance Road it was the most modern of the elementary schools in the town.

Chapter Fourteen

BETWEEN DARNLEY ROAD AND WROTHAM ROAD

THIS CHAPTER TAKES in a square on the south side of Old Road. Starting at the corner of Dashwood Road and Old Road we proceed down Dashwood Road (formerly Dashwood Lane) in a southerly direction, noting on the left Bartlett Road and Lynton Road South, roads constructed in the early 1890s. At the corner of the latter road stood until 1972 a corrugated iron building erected in 1904 and then known as St. Mary's Mission church. After the new church was built in Wrotham Road in 1938 it was used for Sunday school activities and other organisations, but has now been replaced by modern town houses. (The new church and parish will receive attention later.)

Farther on, Woodlands Park, a public recreation meadow stretching to Wrotham Road on the east, is not entirely in Gravesend parish, a wedge-shaped area of Northfleet encroaching upon it and retreating to continue its boundary southward leaving the west side of Dashwood Road within Northfleet borders. On the right stood until 1971 Dashwood House, at one time the house of the Coopers, and later used as Town Planning and other offices. Next door is New House Farm, a pleasant late-18th-century farmhouse, and on the corner stands New House (now offices), both in Northfleet parish.

The roadway at right angles fronting us is New House Lane, and Northfleet parish is to the right. The boundary between the two parishes proceeds southward across fields, so we turn left along New House Lane and then Cross Lane, known until 50 years ago as Cutthroat Lane. At the junction with Meadow Road was a pond. The road now leads to St. George's School, the senior Church of England school of the district, built to meet the need when the older church schools became obsolete. It was opened in February 1939 by the then Bishop of Rochester, the Right Rev. Martin

Linton-Smith. A plaque at the entrance to the school contains these words:

> This school has its origins in the old Gravesend Free School in King Street, founded about 1580 and amalgamated with the National School founded in 1816. In 1932 the site of the combined school in King Street was sold, and out of the public funds provided under the Education Act, 1936, supplemented by the proceeds of the sale of the King Street site the present building was erected.

At the junction of Cross Lane with Upper Wrotham Road we turn to the right in order to bring into this chapter the modern St. Mary's church. The district served by the mission church mentioned above had increased in population since 1904. The roads facing the church, Hillingdon Road, The Fairway, and Dennis Road, were built in the 1930s, and a need was felt for St. Mary's to become a parish in its own right. The new St. Mary's church was consecrated on All Saints Day, 1938, by Dr. Linton-Smith. It cost £6,190. It remained a daughter church of St. George until 1951 when an Order in Council created a separate parish with St. Mary's as the parish church. The new church hall was opened in 1971, but seriously damaged by fire in 1972, and has now been rebuilt.

Retracing our steps to the corner of Cross Lane and wending north, we may remind ourselves that the road we are following was constructed between Gravesend and Borough Green as a turnpike road with toll-gates at intervals in 1825, thus linking Gravesend and Tonbridge via Ightham.

After passing Woodlands Park (the main gates to which are a memorial to George V's Silver Jubilee in 1935) we reach *Woodlands* hotel, which was built in 1896 as a private residence by Mr. George Wood, alderman of the town, when he removed from his residence in East Street, above the brewery which bore his name. The road upon the right slightly farther on, St. Thomas's Avenue, leads to Trosley Avenue, Pinnocks Avenue, and Woodfield Avenue. This last name is derived from the fact that the land between Wrotham

Road and the back gardens of the houses in Singlewell Road was until the close of the 19th century a brickfield owned by a Mr. Wood–who was not the gentleman who built *Woodlands*, but who lived at 'Westfield', Singlewell.

At the junction of Wrotham Road and Old Road stands the almshouses connected with the name of Henry Pinnock. They were built on this site in 1898 to replace those at the corner of King Street and Windmill Street (see Chapter Two), and with funds collected in memory of Prince Albert and for Victoria's Diamond Jubilee. A plaque on the corner front gives particulars of the charity. Extensions were built in 1937, 1951 and 1960. The architects for the original block were F. R. Farrow and B. C. H. Nisbett, and for the extensions, Thorold Bennett.

Previously, there stood here for many years a couple of one-storey thatched dwellings known as 'Reed's Cottages' of late 18th-century date. They belonged to the parish at one time and were used to house cholera victims in the 19th century.

Crossing Old Road, we enter upon Wrotham Road as distinguished from Upper Wrotham Road, although the former name is now used for both lengths. Until the 1950s a ladies' bowling green occupied the north-west corner. Adjoining this and continuing northward are dwelling houses built in the late 19th century at the time that Kent and Essex Roads were cut.

Where Essex Road opens upon Wrotham Road there stood until the 1880s *The Pavilion* theatre and its grounds where, during the summer season, and occasionally during the winter, plays, operas and concerts of a high order were staged. Tragedy overtook its proprietor, Thomas Eves, in 1884 when he was beaten with sticks in the *Pavilion* grounds by two of his youthful employees until he died. The enterprise which he had carried on with such success fell into decay and the building in which the entertainments were presented was sold, and was rebuilt in Milton Road as a volunteer drill hall (see Chapter Ten).

Portland Road, which rises steeply opposite Essex Road, connects at its eastern end with what was formerly known as West Hill, but now is considered part of Windmill Street.

The next chapter will include reference to this southern slope of the hill.

A hundred yards or so farther north along Wrotham Road there stood until 1964 St. Luke's hall. It was built as a 'mission' church of St. James's district in 1890 (architect, Basset-Smith), and served the neighbourhood until the Second World War, after which it found occasional use for meetings connected with the church, and was used for Church Lads' Brigade, Sunday school and similar meetings. The site is now occupied by a Welfare clinic. On its southern side there was erected in 1956 a hut as the training centre and headquarters of the 402 (Gravesend) Squadron Air Training Corps.

Wingfield Road, which dates from the 1880s, recalls the name of Gravesend's first member of parliament, Sir Charles Wingfield, when it received its separate franchise in 1868. The site was before that time known as 'Sandybanks', and was an area of derelict land where youth found amusement in leisure hours. It had previously formed part of Clark's nursery gardens.

Nearly opposite Wingfield Road the Bat and Ball cricket ground was for many years used for county cricket. It seems to have started about 1845 as a private cricket ground for Ruckland House, and in 1853–4 the Earl of Darnley and others formed the North Kent Cricket Club with the Bat and Ball as its home ground. Here the giants of the game have scored some of their great personal successes, Dr. W. G. Grace, Frank Woolley, Kenneth Hutchings, G. Jessop, to name but a few. Lionel Troughton, Kent's Gravesend captain, was also among them. Great consternation was expressed when, after a long history of cricket, the ground was bought in the first decade of the present century by a local builder for building, but a determined effort by individual enthusiasts raised the money for its re-purchase, and the builder, also a Gravesend man, agreed to relinquish it. In 1960 Mr. R. J. Billings gave the Club a 999-year lease at a peppercorn rent. Not only cricket, but bowls, tennis, and more recently, hockey, are played upon its well-kept green.

Trafalgar Road, which borders the cricket ground on its northern side, has, halfway down, standing back within its own grounds, St. James's hospital, which, before the passing of the National Health Act, was the Gravesend and Milton Workhouse, built in 1847 by a Board of Guardians under the Poor Law Act of 1831. Now, re-planned and renovated, it is largely a residence for aged and infirm people.

In Wrotham Road, set high up on the eastern side is Wrotham Road Junior School, built in 1894 as Wrotham Road Board School, the third of such schools built in Gravesend. From this point northwards the houses belong to an earlier date than those on the south, dating from the opening years of the 19th century. Before the erection of of the houses between Wrotham Road and Darnley Road, much of the ground was known as 'Man of Kent Fields', named after the licensed house on the corner of Arthur Street.

The next house to call for notice is the Masonic Hall, which was Ruckland House for many years until it was taken over by the Masonic Order in 1906. Its name recalls its first owner, Lawrence Ruck, a Gravesend grocer and provision merchant of the late 18th century who, with his brother, owned land upon which Ruckland House stands. After his death it was bought by Charles Spencer. Until the close of the 19th century it was the residence of Mrs. Spencer, widow of a chemist, formerly in business in High Street.

Zion Place opposite was so named because it lead to the Zion chapel in Windmill Street of the Baptists, which was built in 1843 (see Chapter Two).

Woodville Terrace has been swept away to make room for the Civic Centre and the police station mentioned in Chapter Two. These houses built in the 1840s stood within their own private road bordered by trees within a low wall mounted by iron railings. Latterly they were used by various departments of the Gravesend council as offices. Albert Place which curved from Wrotham Road into Windmill Street was named after the Prince Consort, and the public house on the corner of Windmill Street was called the *Queen's Arms.* All this has now vanished to make way for the Civic Centre forecourt.

It is at this point in our perambulation that Wrotham Road becomes Stone Street. Wrotham Road, constructed in 1825 as a turnpike highway, was stated to have its beginning in Windmill Street. Before the construction of New Road in 1801, what is now Stone Street was regarded as part of Gravesend Backside (now Princes Street). In 1761 the state of the old main road across the chalk cliff was so dangerous due to quarrying that the Turnpike Trustees decided to take over the road from Queen Mary's Green by John Goldsmith's farmhouse to the Manor Road (i.e., now Pelham Road), and to construct a new road known as Blackberry Lane, along what are now the back gardens on the north side of Cobham Street into Windmill Street. The curved front of the Gravesend Rubber Company's shop and the curved wall beside their office (both demolished 1973) mark the line of this turnpike road which was abandoned and the site of Blackberry Lane sold when the New Road was built by the Trustees in 1801. The stucco-fronted buildings occupied as offices and shops, and now Nos. 21, 22 and 23 Stone Street, were built in 1789 as Gravesend and Milton's workhouse. Before that year, the housing of indigent people was undertaken separately by the respective vestries. The two end buildings were added later and are not part of the workhouse, which can still be clearly identified by the roofs at the rear.

The open square known as Railway Place was in Gravesend's holiday resort period covered by stables for the horses of stage-coaches, and here were also stabled donkeys and goat chaises for the children of visitors. All these were swept away by the coming of the railway in 1849.

On the western side of Stone Street, north of Clive Road, were until comparatively recent years small weatherboard cottages with their own trim-kept gardens enclosed within low wooden palings. Later, they were converted to shops, but one cottage remained until 1953, its last inhabitant, a Mrs. H. Stone, having lived there for 40 years. Beyond was P. E. Lines and Co.'s builders merchants yard. Previously the site was a stable-and-cart yard for tip-carts, and next to the baker, later occupied by the Gravesend Co-operative Society's undertaking department, was a livery and bait stable yard, occupied and run first by Mrs. Houghton in the early 1890 period, and later at the beginning of the 19th century by J. C. Aylen. It was known as the Borough Mews and from here Alfred Joseph Clark ran his horse-bus to Meopham, and on certain days to Cobham, prior to 1914. A second multi-storey car park, opened in 1976, now dominates the west side of Stone Street.

Just before New Road is reached was a store for builders merchants small goods. Previously there was an open space before a building set back somewhat where a hay, straw and fodder merchant carried on business. The building was originally built about 1800 as a hall for the Oddfellows Friendly Society. Later it was the Baptist church until their church was built in Windmill Street in 1843. All this area is now (1973) cleared for redevelopment. The corner bank premises are dealt with in the New Road section (see Chapter Eight).

Chapter Fifteen

PARROCK STREET, PARROCK ROAD AND OLD ROAD

FROM THE BOTTOM of Stone Street, with which the last chapter closes, we proceed to the northern end of Parrock Street where, it will be remembered, Chapter Nine, which dealt with Queen Street, started. Instead of turning left as in that chapter, we turn right, our aim being to include in the present chapter Parrock Street and Parrock Road as far as the Old Road, with reference to the streets lying to the westward of the two former and north of the latter thoroughfare.

First to note upon the right is the low-built house lying back from the road which for many years has been the home of the Conservative Club. It was previously the residence of Evan Lake, Esq., solicitor and member of the Gravesend Corporation. In the early years of the last century its walled garden ran along the south side of King Street (Chapter Eight) for some distance.

Bordering the roadway here and nearer Manor Road there was until the early part of the 19th century, Glover's Pond, so named because a man of that name ended his life by drowning there. It was guarded from the roadway by posts and rails, and details of repair to these are to be found in vouchers of Milton Vestry for the first two decades of the 19th century.

Cromer House, next to the Conservative club, was for many years around the turn of the century the residence of Dr. Firth, who was the first medical man in Gravesend to cover his rounds in a motor-car. He had previously ridden a bicycle of an unusual type, built at a cycle works at Northfleet, which was propelled by an up-and-down movement of the feet, and included one of the first free-wheel devices. During the 1939–45 war, Cromer House became a Y.M.C.A. club for service men stationed in the Gravesend area.

Manor Road was noticed in Chapter Two as a turning out of Windmill Street. The houses beyond, interrupted by the railway, were before its coming to Gravesend, known as Parrock Place, and in one of these houses there died in September 1833, at the age of 76, Jeremiah Lear, the ne'er-do-well father of Edward Lear of *Nonsense Book* fame.

Parallel with Parrock Street to the west and connecting Manor Road with Lord Street was Eden Place (now the site of the multi-storey car park opened in 1972) which in Gravesend's short-lived pleasure resort period was a favourite place of temporary residence for visitors. Lord Street also connects Parrock Street with Windmill Street: its name preserves that of its builder. Leading out of Lord Street to the south was a cul-de-sac, Peppercroft Street, so named from a parcel of land bearing the title of the Peppercrofts. In the early 19th century this site was occupied by a brickfield.

The whole of the area between Parrock Street and the backs of the houses in Windmill Street has been cleared during the last five years. Part of it is now used as a car park and part has been developed with blocks of flats known as Gravesham Court.

The short road now the entrance to the car park was Clarence Street, formerly called Star Street, from the *Star* hotel, which stood on the corner.

Other streets in the area were Union Street, with its extension leading into Windmill Street, bearing the name of South Street. The next upon the right, now the entrance to Gravesham Court, was Russell Street, in which was established in 1851 a day school which served on Sundays as a mission church until 1856, when, Christ Church having been built, it was used as a Sunday school. It continued its day school functions as a Church school and after the passing of the 1902 Education Act was enlarged and improved. It ceased to function as a day school upon the rearrangement of schools in the area in 1936. Clarence Row, its continuation, links up with Windmill Street and still exists, due to the Minister having decided that the houses on its north side built in the grounds of Clarence House school should remain when the area was cleared in 1965.

Still farther south were John Street, Peter Street and William Street, commemorating members of the family of Mr. L. P. Staff, mayor of the town in 1843, who was interested in the erection of the houses there. Opposite the junction of William Street and Parrock Street is an open space enclosed within the 'close' of Christ Church Crescent with Christ Church Road nearby. In the centre, some blocks of masonry remain as a reminder that here stood for 80 years from 1856 the former Christ church, which was built at a time when the population of Gravesend was extending southward in this direction. The architect was R. C. Carpenter, who died while it was being built, and it was completed by William Slater. The church was for many years the 'parade' church for troops occupying Milton barracks nearby. Deterioration of structure necessitated the closing of the church on 3 December 1932. The church was taken down and rebuilt in Old Road East (see Chapter Seventeen).

It is at this point that Parrock Street becomes Parrock Road, but before making our way along it it will be well to cross Clarence Place (see Chapter One) and ascend the somewhat steeper incline of Shrubbery Road which leads to the east side of Windmill Hill (see Chapter One). A little distance along this road on the right are two public houses. The first, now called *The Windmill Tavern* was originally a farmhouse dating from the 18th century, and is mentioned in Pocock's *History* as the farm to the north of Windmill Hill. The second, called *The Miller's Cottage,* was once the residence of the miller when milling activities were conducted at the mill. It was considerably extended in 1973.

Nearly opposite the *Windmill Tavern* is the romantically-named Primrose Terrace set high on the side of the hill, the back entrances to these houses being in Southill Road, which descends into Parrock Road. At a still higher level at the very top of the hill is Constitution Crescent, a row of four stucco-fronted houses, some of which have recently been restored and which form a landmark visible for many miles. Where the ground falls away to the east the road becomes Southill Road and in the triangle now occupied by modern town houses were a number of buildings in 'rustic' brick at one time 'The Shrubbery' tea gardens. The house, known as 'The Shrubbery', was in the early years of the 20th century occupied by Charles Cobham, a local architect and collector of local histories and guide-books. He was also one of Gravesend's pioneer motorists. This area before the erection of houses, was rough ground with sand and gravel pits, and in a hovel composed of boughs and odd timber dwelt an old fortune-teller, whose clients were the visitors to the Hill. A footway from the east side of Constitution Crescent leads to Constitution Hill, which also opens out on to Parrock Road.

It will be well to retrace our steps again now to the point at which the deviation from Parrock Road began, and proceed along it in order that we may observe the open view to the north-east over Harmsworth's sports ground, with Milton church in the middle distance (Chapter Ten), to the lower part of Gravesend Reach, the Lower Hope, and the head of Sea Reach. Attractive and stimulating at all times except when weather conditions limit vision, this wide scene is at its best in the evening of a summer day when it is bathed in sunshine and the long shadows of houses in the background fall across the nearer ground. Those who built the houses set high above the road saw the great advantage of their site at a time when in the early- and mid-19th century fleets of sailing ships filled the river's tideway. Some of these houses built about 1840 were named Bronte Villas, probably from Nelson, who was Viscount Nelson and Bronte.

As we proceed southward passing Constitution Hill, it may be noted that it was at the point where it joins Parrock Road that the first pumping works of the Gravesend and Milton waterworks, built in 1833, stood, before their removal to the site on the south of Windmill Hill. This is now Rowland Lodge. On the opposite corner is 'Echo Cottage', where it is said that Louis Napoleon (L'Aiglon) stayed under the name of 'Mr. Smith' when he was in living in England prior to the revolution of 1848.

The next turning upon the right is Leith Park Road, which leads to the Gravesend pumping station of the waterworks, built in 1846 to replace the original pumping station in Parrock Road, and demolished in 1973. The square chimney was a well-known landmark. Until about 1890 water was only pumped at certain hours of the day and most of the older houses in the town had large storage tanks which were a source of trouble in frosty weather. Running south from this road opposite the waterworks was a cul-de-sac, Glen View, which commands a view over the western countryside towards Swanscombe Woods and beyond. The end of this road now leads to the new estate on the site of Milton Mount college, and town houses and the new houses of the Southwark Rescue Society now cover much of this side of the hill. At the end of what is now Glen View on Three Tree Hill stood a brick-built tower windmill, which was pulled down at the end of the 18th century for the bricks.

Formerly, Parrock Road was narrow with barely two carriage-widths between Southill Road and Old Road East, large elm trees bordering it on the eastern side. These were left in the centre when a second roadway was constructed about 1910, but they were all felled in the 1930s and flowering trees planted. Near the junction with Echo Square (so called because of a remarkable echo to be heard there before much building altered acoustic response) there stood until 1972 on a high bank a building known for many years as Milton Mount college. It was founded as an educational institution for the daughters of Congregational ministers, although other pupils were accepted from an early date. The foundation stone was laid in 1871. It remained as such until the 1914–18 war, when it moved to Crawley, where it continued until after the 1939–45 war. When the school left the building was used first as a hostel for Vickers' munition workers, and later for a time as a hospital for invalid soldiers. In 1921 it was sold for an orphan school run by Roman Catholic educational authorities, and continued as part of the Southwark Rescue Society. During the 1939–45 war it was occupied by the Auxiliary (later National) Fire Service and the Women's Voluntary Service as a canteen. After the war the Southwark Rescue Society returned, but carried on their work in new buildings and houses built in the grounds which stretched to Leith Park Road. After remaining empty for some time it was demolished in 1972 and the site developed for housing.

At Echo Square we turn to the right along Old Road in order that the stretch of road between Parrock Road and Windmill Street may be covered. (The south side of the road will be dealt with in a later chapter.) On the right is a high wall built with a type of hexagonal artificial brick made up of granite chippings set in a brick surround with cement. It has not been possible to identify this type of material, but it is believed to have been imported from France. In its centre a long flight of stone steps lead to Milton Court (now demolished; the site was excavated, 1974/75), built high on the south slope of the hill. This house, known for many years as 'Simpson's Folly', was built by William Simpson after he had vacated a house at Rosherville, known as 'Chiltern Lodge', following a dispute with the Gardens authorities whose London Road tower, so he alleged, invaded the privacy of his garden. The architects were Parr and Strong.

At the junction of Spring Grove with Old Road East there stood until 1971 a house known as 'Glenthorne', latterly used as the Convent Grammar school. It was at one time the residence of John Russell, alderman and brewer of the town, and had a tunnel under Old Road which connected with extensive gardens running down to Cross Lane. A later owner built a new house, 'Glendillon', on this garden, and this is now used as Milton Mount United Reformed church. It was opened as a Congregational church in 1953, when Princes Street and Clarence Place churches closed. Milton Court also had a garden on the south side of Old Road enclosed with a wall of similar material to that on the north side.

On the corner of Old Road East and Windmill Street is the *Prince of Orange* inn, rebuilt on the site of an old coaching house of the 18th century, with a history going back into the 17th century. It was the coaching inn for London to Dover coaches which used the old road prior to the cutting of New Road in 1801 (see Chapter Eight), after which all coaches passed through the centre of the town. When these changes took place, an inn at the top of High Street became known as the *'New' Prince of Orange* and the Old Road inn became the *'Old' Prince of Orange,* the licensee moving from one to the other. Adjoining the *Old Prince of Orange* was at one time a cricket ground.

The area bounded by Parrock Street, King Street and Old Road East has now been surveyed with the exception of the south part of Windmill Street, known for many years as West Hill. It is necessary, therefore, to turn north and deal briefly with this length of thoroughfare. On the right is the western end of Leith Park, spoken of earlier in this chapter, and just beyond, within its own grounds, stood until 1967 a residence which was witness to an ambitious scheme of building never completed. It was the dream of William Aspdin, who claimed to be the inventor of Portland cement (see Northfleet). He enclosed a large area between Windmill Street, Leith Park Road and Sandybank Road with a high concrete wall with large gate towers and entrances, parts of which still exist, and intended to build an extensive country house to be known as 'Portland House', of which plans and illustrations exist. 'West Hill House' as built was only a fragment of this. Aspdin got into financial difficulties and the remaining part of the estate was developed with houses now known as West Hill and Sunnyside, and the eastern part was bought by the Water Company. Town houses now occupy the site of 'West Hill House'.

As we pass Portland Road (see Chapter Fourteen) 'Berkley House' on the left was formerly a High School for Ladies, and opposite it, set high on the slope of the hill, are houses erected during the 1930s, where once were the gardens of the popular *Tivoli* hotel (see Chapter One). A plan for the layout of the *Tivoli* site may be seen in the Gravesend Reference Library. Before the various buildings were erected on the side of the hill and until the first decade of the 19th century was a building known as 'The Blew House'.

It was here that in our first chapter we moved northwards.

Chapter Sixteen

BETWEEN PARROCK STREET AND WELLINGTON STREET

BEFORE 1840 THE TRIANGLE having Parrock Street, Milton Road and Wellington Street was open farming or market garden ground, but the remarkable growth of population in Milton, which rose from 2,769 in 1821 to 9,927 in 1851, caused speculators in real estate to cast covetous eyes on the area with a consequence that the roads within the triangle, Edwin Street, The Grove, Peacock Street, and Wellington Street, were cut and houses erected. The Milton Park Estate Company which had developed Harmer Street had as its directors members of the City of London Corporation, and these extended their efforts south of Milton Road, giving their names to some of the streets.

If we take as our starting-point the junction of Milton Road and Parrock Street as we did in our last chapter, and crossing to the east side walk up Parrock Street we shall pass the Roman Catholic church mentioned in Chapter Ten, and after a few yards reach the wall which guards the length of line laid down in the mid-19th century to connect the systems of the Gravesend and Rochester railway and the North Kent railway (see Chapter Twelve). Bordering this railway cutting on its southern side is Saddington Street, a name which was not given to it until late in the 19th century. Before this it was Farringdon Street, and was so named became James Harmer, a leading figure in the development of Gravesend (see Chapter Ten) was Alderman of Farringdon Ward in the City of London. Its later name connects it with another City alderman, a clothier named Saddington.

If we turn along this street we arrive at the first intersection, Edwin Street, another commemoration of City of London association, Alderman Edwin, who was interred in St. George's churchyard (see Chapter Five), having been also a City Corporation member. At a little distance up Edwin Street on the right the roadway opens into Parrock Street and makes with that street a smaller triangle at the apex of which stands a public house, *The Little Wonder,* more colloquially known as 'the flat iron' because of its wedge shape.

We turn to the left over the railway bridge and note on the east side of Edwin Street, near Milton Road, a low-built structure which has been in the course of years the town's post office, a Y.M.C.A. club, the offices of the *Gravesend and Dartford Reporter,* and the 'Medical Hall' —so-called from its being part of a chemist's premises in Milton Road used as a hall for meetings, concerts, parties, etc.

From this point we walk the few yards to The Grove along Milton Road. The Grove was first called Harmer Street South, or Upper Harmer Street, it being the original intention of its planners to continue the architectural treatment of Harmer Street to the south of Milton Road (see Chapter Ten). When it was re-planned as a series of semi-detached villas, it was for a time a private road with gates at each end. Changes which have taken place since their erection have introduced office and business premises to The Grove, the post office having brought within its area the lower houses on the east side. Two large office blocks, one on each side of the road, now occupy most of the remaining frontage between the post office and the railway. The block on the east, Stephenson House, built in 1965, now houses the Inspector of Taxes office (moved from Lynton House in 1969) and the offices of the Department of National Health and Social Security (moved from Ravenscourt in Pelham Road at the end of 1972) on the opposite side.

One important change is in the character of the large house just beyond Saddington Street, which was throughout the 19th century a large day and boarding school for boys, 'Hedger's'. After remaining empty for some time it was taken over by a laundry company.

On the left-hand side near the top of The Grove on a site immediately to the south of St. Andrew's Road stood St.

Andrew's Presbyterian Church of England, established in 1870 from a congregation which worshipped for a time in the town hall. It was built at a cost of £5,000 and had twin spires at the west end when built. It was demolished in 1965, but some of the stained glass was removed to St. Paul's church, its successor in Singlewell Road.

St. Andrew's Road leads to Peacock Street, a name not associated in any way with the bird of splendid plumage, but again preserving the name of another director of the building company, Mr. Deputy Peacock of the City Corporation, a Bishopsgate baker. A public house with the title *The Peacock* stands on the corner of St. Andrew's Road. On the right, Peacock Street does not join with Parrock Street as do the earlier streets noted, but runs into Waterloo Street, a roadway which led to Milton barracks.

Once again we turn left down Peacock Street, and crossing Saddington Street, proceed in the direction of Milton Road, in order to observe what was at one time a school where a good-class commercial and general education for boys was obtainable, known as Smith's Modern School. Now the premises of a printer and bookbinder, it was originally opened as Milton British School, an elementary school for Nonconformist children, who otherwise had to attend one of the Church schools, education by the State not having been sponsored as today. It was after it was taken over by Mr. C. Hooper Smith, who had been appointed headmaster about 1874, that its reputation rose so rapidly and so justifiably, and tuition at the school was eagerly sought by parents for their sons. As higher standards of education were attained by State schools towards the close of the 19th century, privately-run schools were less patronised, and after 'Gaffer' Smith had relinquished his interest in the Middle Class school, which was later conducted by H. Waldegrave, it was closed and became for a time a dancing academy run by Mr. and Mrs. Freeborn. Then for a time it was a repertory theatre and survived the Second World War as *The Playhouse*, but its fortunes fluctuated and it was closed in 1950 and has since been occupied by Lewis and Sons, printers.

Wellington Street is the next and last street in this group. For many years until the early part of the 20th century Walker's Wellington Brewery stood on the east side just north of the railway. This was acquired by the large London brewery firm of Charrington's, who continued brewing there, but this was discontinued about 1928, and later the building was demolished and the site used as part of *The Jolly Drayman,* better known as the 'Brewery Tap', or colloquially as 'the Coke Oven' in Love Lane. Charrington's still have their offices on the west side of Wellington Street opposite the old brewery site.

Parallel with Wellington Street on its eastern side, with the high wall of the former Barracks on one side and the back gardens of the houses in Wellington Street on the other, is a wide passage that in earlier years justified its title of Love Lane. With open country views over sloping ground towards the river on one side and the aspect of the town on the other, it ran between low hedges from Milton Road to the base of Windmill Hill, and was much favoured by youth of both sexes for sociable perambulation. The title of Love Lane was bestowed upon it as a nickname, it being first known as Gurnett's Walk, from having been a public gift in perpetuity to the town of Gravesend by Thomas Gurnett 'to provide a pleasant walk to Windmill Hill from Milton Place'. In addition to the previously-mentioned names, it was also known as Pennywick Lane, Pennycoat Lane (a variant of Petticoat Lane), and as Melancholy Walk. That it was a popular path to Windmill Hill is provable by a voucher of Milton Vestry expenditure of 1830. 'Paid to W. Webster, To writing 144 inches on the gable end of Mr Amos's house "Love Lane leading to Windmill Hill" at ½d per inch, 6/-. To painting ground 1/6.'.

Milton barracks were built in 1863 on land purchased from the South Eastern Railway Company in 1860. It was occupied by various regiments, and in summertime was the quarters of troops undergoing musketry training, who marched in columns of four to the butts at Shorne Mead. It was finally closed in 1971.

Chapter Seventeen

MILTON AND PARROCK MANOR HOUSES AND ENVIRONS

THIS CHAPTER DEALS with the area bounded on the north by Parrock Avenue, on the west by Parrock Road, on the south by Old Road East, and on the east by Denton parish. Assuming that the perambulation set out in the previous chapter ended at the top of Wellington Street or Love Lane, only a few yards of Parrock Road have to be covered before the north-west corner of the area is reached, the top of Parrock Avenue. Most of the houses here are modern, and within a comparatively few years it was pastureland or farmland.

First of all, however, mention must be made of Plum Pudding Lane, a pathway leading from Parrock Road to Church Walk (see Chapter Ten) on the north side of Parrock Avenue. This was as much sought after 50 years ago by courting couples as was Love Lane 80 years earlier. Meadowland stretched from Parrock Road, guarded by an iron fence down to a large house, which in the 1890s was known as 'The Home Boys', it being the hostel of an organisation connected with the Homes for Little Boys at Farningham, elder lads being employed upon the farm and a dairy business carried on with the house as centre.

Actually, 'The Home Boys' was the manor house of the manor of Milton, and it still stands, a large 18th-century house in Joy Road, let out into flats, still preserving some of the features which graced it when it was built in 1761 by Peter Moulson, then lord of the manor of Milton. Milton Manor House was known at various times as 'Figges', 'Sir Thomas Wyatt's Place', 'Milton Place', and, quite erroneously as 'Lower Parrock'. In the early 19th century the present house was the property of, and was occupied by, Thomas Dalton, a colonel in the West Kent Militia, and Groom of the Bedchamber to the Duke of Gloucester, who was commander of the regiment. It was here that Col. Dalton entertained the Duke, his officers and men when the regiment returned from service on the Continent after the Napoleonic Wars. Col. Dalton (who died in 1827, and to whom there is a tablet in Milton church) was the last lord of the manor to reside in the manor house, the manor becoming the property on his death of members of the Raphael family (although the house was sold elsewhere). Richard Barham, author of *Ingoldsby Legends*, frequently stayed here with Col. Dalton, of whose property he was an executor, and it was during his visits that he wrote some of the poems which have a local reference. (Cruden's *History of Gravesend* [1843] contains much of interest regarding the manor of Milton, including some farm accounts of the 14th century.)

There is yet another manor house within the area dealt with in this chapter, that of Parrock, to whose owner in 1268, Robert de la Parrok, was granted a market and fair. It is this charter which is referred to in an inscription at the entrance to Gravesend market today (see Chapter Two), the Corporation of Gravesend having bought the manor of Parrock from George Etkins in 1694. The de Gravesend family, members of which became Bishops of Lincoln and of London, were lords of the manor of Parrock in the 14th century and may have resided there in the manor house of that time.

The present Parrock Manor is approached from Echo Square and its south front encases a timber-framed block of two storeys with attics built 1620–1630. There is a brick chimney at each end and a fine chimney-piece with shouldered arch, floral spandrils and a lintel ornamented with paterae and halved Tudor roses. That at the other end was the kitchen. On the first floor is a similar fireplace of simpler type. The present false front was added about 1775. In 1830 a large new block, now known as Parrock Manor or 'North House' was added. It has a porch with Tuscan columns and a low slate roof with deep eaves. The old 'Byre House' is now two residences, and until 1952 there existed a barn, relic of the days when the property was known as Parrock farm. An interesting detached weather-boarded building in the grounds of the old manor may be a granary.

In the 16th century the old manor house of Parrock was known as 'Spryvers Hache', a name that has an echo of a deed of 1456 which refers to the house of John Sprever which stood where now the old town hall stands in High Street, with the market behind. The manor of Parrock does not appear to have possessed a continuous area of landed property, its holdings being scattered in the parish of Milton.

Christ church, Milton, is the successor of the earlier Christ church mentioned in Chapter Fifteen. Much of the material from the old church was taken down, marked and erected on the new site. The architect of the new church was G. E. Clay. The foundation stone was laid by Florence Dowager Countess of Darnley on 16 October 1934, and the church was consecrated on 14 September 1935.

On the rising ground to the east of the district, where now Pine Avenue and Milton Hall Road are built, there stood from 1863 to 1930 the mansion built by George Matthews Arnold, solicitor and mayor of Gravesend eight times, bearing the name of Milton Hall (architect, Geo. Summers Clarke). In its extensive grounds Mr. Arnold established a museum of antiquities in which were housed objects of local interest, including prehistoric flint implements excavated from chalk quarries in the neighbourhood, fossils, Roman remains from Springhead and Higham, and various articles with local historical associations. These, after Mr. Arnold's death in 1908, were dispersed, some finding a place in the Maidstone museum, others in Gravesend public library, in whose reference library some of the documents are housed. Mr. Arnold was also the donor of two statues of Queen Victoria to the town, and of land near the river for the extension of Gravesend promenade and the Gordon Memorial gardens (see Chapters Two, Twelve and Thirteen). Pine Avenue was the drive which lead to the mansion and the first house on the west side, now much altered was the Lodge. In the back garden of 30 Pine Avenue are the columns of the old Gravesend market, presented to G. M. Arnold in 1898 when the present market hall was erected.

PART THREE

Chapter Eighteen

MILTON PARISH SOUTH OF OLD ROAD EAST

WE START THIS CHAPTER at the junction of Old Road with Windmill Street on the north and Singlewell Road on the south, reminding ourselves again that the parishes of Gravesend and Milton have their boundaries along these thoroughfares. While we are waiting for the traffic lights to change (and at this corner were the first traffic lights erected in Gravesend in 1929), the not-so-old may glance obliquely to the left down Devonshire Road and reflect that this and Central Avenue into which the former leads follow roughly a path across cornfields to Singlewell, which was a favourite summer evening walk until the early years of the 20th century. Here until 1929 was the terminus of the Windmill Street tram service, and at an earlier date the turning point of the donkey rides from the *Tivoli*.

We cross to Singlewell Road, known for many years until building increased as Singlewell Lane, a narrower roadway than now, and less well kept as regards its surface. The first houses in Singlewell Road were those on the west side which, together with the cottages running south from Hammonds Corner, were built from 1883 onwards. The row on the east side were not built until 1906 and were one of the earliest blocks in the town to have electric light installed when built, but some of them had gaslight as well as a precaution against current failures. It was in the back garden of No. 12 that the twin-chamber Denehole, described in Philips' *History* was found in 1905 and opened up again after the floods of 1958.

At the beginning of the 19th century there stood on the north-west corner of Cross Lane Mount Pleasant, the residence of James Leigh Joynes, brewer, banker, estate-developer, whose enterprise was responsible for the planning and building of The Terrace (see Chapter Nine). Outbuildings occupied part of the Cross Lane frontage, and meadowland, with small plantations of trees, backed the whole as far as Old Road to which there was a carriage drive. Unfortunately Mr. Joynes's incursions into so many business fields led to financial misfortune, and Mount Pleasant and its surrounding buildings were sold to Col. Thomas Dalton (see Chapter Seventeen), who already owned a large proportion of the land southwards from Old Road. Col. Dalton demolished the house about 1822 and turned the estate into market garden land.

On the east side of Singlewell Road there stood until just before the First World War a large area of glasshouses belonging to Frank Badman, nurseryman and gardener, known as Cemetery Nurseries, but these were gradually diminished to make way for the houses which now stand between Old Road and Cross Lane. The last fragment of this nursery survived until about 1950 when it was built on.

For older Gravesenders, the right-hand corner of Cross Lane and Singlewell Road will always be Hammond's Corner, for here, from 1884 until 1967, was the bakery and sweet shop established by Humphrey Hammond, formerly the manager of a bakery at the corner of Bath Street, now owned by Mr. Frank Smith. The business was continued by his son, Herbert Charles Hammond (who died in 1967), and two daughters, the latter of whom died in 1975, and the shop is for sale. The opposite corner was until about 1905 occupied by the playing fields of Gutteridge's school.

From this corner the road rises southward until Watling Street, known to motorists as A2 or M2, is reached a mile farther south. The row of cottages on the west side ends with a parade of shops built in 1934, and thereafter three roads, Hillingdon Road, The Fairway, and Dennis Road, link Singlewell Road with Upper Wrotham Road.

Beyond these roads is the 18-hole course of the Mid-Kent Golf Club, which at one time extended northwards as far as the Central Parade, the old clubhouse being on the east side of Singlewell Road at the corner of Ascot Road. Across the southern part of the golf course the former southern boundary of the parish of Gravesend runs from the 'hamlet of Claphall' in Upper Wrotham Road to Gypsy Corner at both ends of which the old parish boundary stones can still be seen. A very pleasant loop roadway between Gypsy Corner and Ridgeway Avenue still remains to remind present-day citizens of the quiet, narrow lane to Singlewell which preceded the modern road (built in 1920). The parish boundary continued across fields as far as Lamorna Avenue, the land farther south both in Gravesend and Milton being portions of the parishes of Northfleet and Ifield previous to 1935.

At this point it is well to return to Hammond's Corner, and sketch lightly the developments on the east of Singlewell Road between it and the next north-south road, Whitehill Road. The first on the left (Portland Avenue issues from Cross Lane) is Ferndale Road, and at its intersection with Central Avenue is St. Faith's Hall, which before the building of the new Christ church was a 'mission' church opened in 1906 for that part of Milton parish south of Old Road East. It was closed in 1935, when the new Christ church was opened, and has since been used for parochial activities of a social nature as well as for meetings of associations having social welfare as their aim. It has been replaced (1975) by a new hall adjoining Christ church, and is to be demolished. Between Singlewell Road and Sun Lane is a maze of residential roads served by two licensed houses, *Central Avenue* hotel and *General Gordon* hotel, the latter keeping in remembrance Gordon's association with the town (see Chapter Five), two schools, Kings Farm primary in Cedar Avenue, and Southfields secondary, near to Singlewell Road, and two sports grounds of large extent. The whole of the area between Old Road East on the north, Sun Lane on the east, the boundary line of Milton with Northfleet on the south, and Singlewell Lane on the west, was known in the late 18th century as Punchbowl Field. In the early 19th century when it was the duty of 'highway surveyors' to compel property owners to repair the roads of the parish (or pay a highway rate), the southern part of this area was the source of much material in the form of flints which were carted from King's Farm and Christian's Fields, two names which still survive, and laid as foundations of the thoroughfares in the older part of the town.

With the exception of the western end of Portland Avenue and Ferndale Road, which were opened before the First World War, all these roads were laid out and built up in the 1920s and 1930s. The area was known as Craggs Farm (although the farmhouse was in Singlewell) and was developed by the Gravesend Land Company on land bought from the Raphael family in 1907.

Kings Farm Estate was the first council estate built to re-house the inhabitants of the area between Church Street and West Street, when this area was demolished under slum clearance. The land was bought by the Corporation in 1919 and the first council houses were erected at the top of Whitehall Road and in Sun Lane and Cornwall Avenue and Jellicoe Avenue were cut and houses built in the early 1920s.

The area became part of Christ Church parish in 1935 and a new church, the Church of the Holy Family, was built to serve this area and dedicated by Bishop H. C. Read in June 1959.

The next perambulation of this southern part of the parish of Milton starts at Echo Square. Here it will be noted that two roads run south, Whitehill Road and Sun Lane. Of these Sun Lane is the older, having been originally a lane leading to Cobham; it joins into Whitehill Road again at the top and beyond this point southward was known until shortly after the Second World War as Whitehill Lane or 'the lane to the Sanatorium'. At the junction of Sun Lane and Cross Lane there stood until about 1900 a building formerly the *Sun* inn or beerhouse, from which the lane took its name. To this Pocock refers in his *Chronology*, where he records that a suicide named Knight was buried 'in the four-went way near the Sun public-house, now a private house' (1797). It is worth noting that Pocock records a four-went way where there are now six. Whitehill Road was a footpath until 1853, and Old Road joined Cross Lane at the western end of Elnathan Cottages prior to 1795, when the turnpike commissioners altered the road to its present course and later sold the 'sandbank' between the roads and the cottages were built in 1884. Sun Lane was also called 'Old Sun Lane' and 'Sun Pond Lane', the latter from the pond shown in old maps which was in the depression on the right-hand side near the end of Portland Avenue. About three-quarters of the way along Whitehill Road on the right beyond Canterbury Road may be seen a pair of tall iron gates leading to an enclosure where formerly stood the residence of Mr. G. E. Sharland, town clerk of Gravesend for many years. These gates stood prior to 1901 at the London Road entrance to Rosherville Gardens. On the opposite side of the road stood Canterbury House, at one time the residence of W. Edmonds, a dentist, who was a one-time mayor and alderman. This was the first house to have electric light from current generated by a small steam engine installed by his son Hubert Edmonds, a marine engineer.

The houses in Sun Lane (east side) and Whitehill Road date from the middle of the 19th century with later ones filling the gaps and replacing some of the older houses, which had large gardens.

On the left of Whitehill Road, Laurel Avenue and Hollybush Road lead to a maze of new residential roads similar to that between Whitehill Road and Singlewell Road, most of which date from the 1930s and some of which are of post-Second World War construction.

Several deneholes have been found in this area, including a large one at the rear of the *Echo* public house, on a site now occupied by garages.

To close this chapter we return to Echo Square in order to complete the survey of Old Road East within the Milton territory leading to Denton, and note on the right-hand side The Drive, at the end of which is St. Joseph's convent and chapel, which was formerly 'Hillside', the residence of Mr. John Russell, alderman and brewer of the town, and built by him about 1880 on a small spur with views over both the river to the north and the open country to the south.

Chapter Nineteen

THE PARISH OF DENTON

THE PARISH OF DENTON, which from 1895 had been part of Strood Rural District Council, became part of the Borough of Gravesend in 1935, and has almost lost its identity as streets within its boundaries are continued into the parishes of Milton and Chalk: but the fact that this volume is concerned with the historical as well as the topographical aspect of the township demands that an account be given of the boundaries of the old parish and its principal features as well as a brief survey of its past.

From north to south, Denton is long as compared with its breadth, its west and east limits ending in a point towards the south-east, similar to the tip of a pen. Its western boundary is also the eastern boundary of Milton, as its eastern boundary is that also of Chalk on the western side of that parish. Like all riverside parishes it extends theoretically into the centre of the Thames, its shore on the north being a matter of about 1,000 yards from a point west of 'Woodville Cottages' (built in 1883, but most of which have recently been demolished), to a spot beyond the Port of London Isolation Hospital to the east (closed 1974). From the western point the parish boundary crosses the railway and runs to the north of Waterton Avenue, and follows Elliott Street to the London-Rochester road, where it swings round in a south-easterly direction towards Rochester. Thence in a south-south-westerly direction to Hillside and Lamorna Avenue, which it follows to cross Valley Drive and make the pen-point mentioned above. The eastern boundary runs roughly north from this point, leaving St. Dunstan's Drive and part of Hampton Crescent within the parish to Old Road East, where it turns along the road to the junction with Rochester Road and thence skirts Ingoldsby Road and pursues a somewhat zigzag course which is dictated by the marsh ditches to the riverside again below the hospital. Within the borders of Denton parish on the marshes is Gravesend Corporation Sewage Disposal Works, main drainage being installed in the 1930s.

Like the southern portion of Gravesend, Milton and Chalk, the southern portion of Denton has been thickly built over. Until the 1930s the only part occupied by domestic dwellings consisted of a number of short streets on the north side of the London-Rochester Road. Lower Range Road was the most important of these, gaining its name from the fact that it was by this road that troops housed in Milton barracks proceeded to the butts at Shorne Mead for musketry practice. An inn at the turn of the road is called *The Markers' Retreat.* A school, Denton primary, stands at the corner where Empress Road leads from Lower Range Road and was built to cater for Denton and Chalk when they lay outside the Borough. Where now is Baltimore Terrace there was formerly a group of weatherboard dwellings known as 'the five houses'. One of these was in the 1890s the cottage-shop of 'Mother Kirk', whose home-made toffee, manufactured in little patty-pans, was one of the locally appreciated sweetmeats. A little farther along on the left was the prosperous dairy of W. J. Champion (now the United Dairies office), a staunch supporter of Milton church nearby, his son, Harold, being for some years its talented organist, who also had the organ renovated in 1936 at his own expense.

A little farther along on the left-hand side, its west wall only a few yards from the footway, is a Roman Catholic chapel, built by G. M. Arnold on the site of the former parish church of Denton: the ruins of this ancient church were incorporated in the newer edifice. (Reference to this church and the manor of Denton will be found in the historical matter at the end of this chapter.)

Until 1936 there stood to the south-east of the chapel Denton Court, built in 1791 by Nicholas Gilbee, on the site of the ancient manor house of Denton. On the demolition of Denton Court the site was cleared for building, the name surviving in Denton Court Road which occupies part of the site. Mr. Gilbee also built a smock windmill on the waterside on a site adjoining 'Woodville Cottages' about 1790 as well as building a wharf there. The mill was pulled down towards the end of the 19th century. Until the withdrawal of the passenger service to Allhallows in 1961 there was a Denton Halt (opened in 1906), immediately to the east of the level crossing, at which these trains stopped. A prominent feature of the marshes is now the National Sea Training School and the new mission centre of the Mission to Seamen. The school was moved here in 1967. The architects were Lyons, Israel, Ellis and Partners.

The earliest reference to Denton in documents is to be found in a will of 950 A.D., in which Byrtric, a Saxon thane of Meopham and his wife, Aelfswythe, bequeathed land at Denetune in order that masses might be said for the souls of himself and his parents. Domesday Book 1086 A.D. refers to Danitone and its church, and at intervals during the following two centuries the manor, its dues and possessions are set out in various documents. The Domesday spelling of the name has played a part in the belief that it refers to possession at some time by Danish settlers (Dane town), but modern philologists favour the derivation from 'denu', a Saxon word for valley.

With the very small and probably decreasing population that Denton had it is not surprising to learn that services ceased to be held in Denton parish church after 1650 in the Commonwealth period. No record of a priest holding the living is existent after the incumbency of John Stace in 1536. Burials continued in the churchyard until 1678, but the ecclesiastical parish was no longer a reality: its revenues appear to have accrued to the diocese until 1879 when part of them was allotted to the rector of Milton, presumably a recognition of his spiritual responsibility for inhabitants of Denton. The adjoining parish of Chalk came to be recognised as being the church for banns of marriage, etc., in the late 18th century and the early 19th century, the registers of 1788 referring to a bridegroom as being 'of the extra-parochial place of Denton', and another as being of 'Denton, having no church or chapel standing'.

The old churchyard of Denton extended in a westerly direction, including land through which the present roadway on the Milton side was cut when the 'turnpike', now Rochester Road, was made. The ruins of this church were the site of the imaginary Ingoldsby Abbey in the Rev. R. H. Barham's poem where 'A full choir of monks and a full choir of nuns shall live upon cabbage and hot cross buns'. Ingoldsby Road and Abbey Road derive their names from this poem in the *Ingoldsby Legends.*

Further particulars of the parish are to be found in *Denton,* by G. M. Arnold, a copy of which can be seen in Gravesend public library.

Mention should be made in this section of the vast housing estates on either side of Valley Drive, all built since the Second World War. The upper part of Valley Drive was formerly part of Whitehall Lane and on its east side were the isolation hospitals and sanitorium of Gravesend and Strood councils (built in 1887), Denton and Chalk parishes both being formerly part of Strood Rural District. A proposal to use these hospitals for a maternity hospital is commemorated in the name of a public house established in one of the former hospital buildings and called *The Stork at Rest.*

Chapter Twenty

THE PARISH OF CHALK

AS LATE AS THE EARLY YEARS of the 20th century Chalk was a village remote and separate from Gravesend. Its few houses on the old main road to Rochester and the sparsely-set cottages and farmhouses on the Lower Road to Higham were only seen by those Gravesend inhabitants who indulged in a Sunday afternoon walk in that direction, or by youthful cyclists and later motorists out for a country spin. Taken into the Gravesend Corporation area in 1935, Chalk has become, so far as its south-western portion is concerned, a huge housing estate. The former Gravesend airport opened as the Gravesend School of Flying in 1932, from which Amy Johnson started her record flight and which became a war-time fighter station, was sold to Dolphin Development in 1957, and is now covered by the River View Park Estate.

Most of the traffic through Chalk passes along the wide highway constructed between Gravesend and Strood in 1921 under one of the Unemployment Relief Acts. This leaves the former village road on the left and only joins it to absorb it about seven-eighths of a mile farther east. It we take this older road at the roundabout, which has just (1972) been completed, we pass a building which was formerly the malting premises of Charrington's brewery (its twin towers were taken down in 1957). It is now devoted to educational purposes. Almost opposite was the Chalk tollgate, set up by the Turnpike Commissioners who, under a series of local acts, the first of which was granted in 1711, maintained the main road between Northfleet (later extended to Dartford) and Strood. The site of the Chalk gate was originally further east, but was moved to this spot when the road was straightened in 1777. The turnpike trust was wound up in 1871 when the County took over responsibility for this main road. On the right of the road at the corner of Forge

Lane, which in older days extended southward to the extreme southern boundary of the parish, is the forge from which Charles Dickens drew some of the features of the forge in his novel *Great Expectations.* A small notice board on the house adjoining chronicles this fact. Oscar Mullender, the last smith to operate the smithy, knew Dickens well. Opposite a lane leads down to 'West Court', a pleasant 18th-century house, and one of the Chalk manors, and then to the marshes. A little farther on stood the former *White Hart* inn, a new inn with the same name having been built on the newer road some distance in the rear. Chalk at one time, and as late as the beginning of the 20th century, boasted another inn in the village street, *The Lord Nelson*: this has been closed and demolished some years ago. It stood near the junction of Lower Higham Road.

The village school building has now been demolished and replaced by a hall used mainly for social functions and the youth club.

Just past the junction of the road to the left which leads to Higham, Cliffe and other hamlets in the Hundred of Hoo, is a cottage on which there is a bust of Charles Dickens, by Fitzgerald, with a tablet stating that it was here that Dickens spent his honeymoon. The tablet was erected by the local Dickens Fellowship in 1912. This house is usually known as 'Craddock's Cottage', from the name of the 19th-century tenant, who let lodgings and was 'identified' as the honeymoon cottage by the late Mr. A. J. Philip. Previously the house at the corner of Vicarage Lane, now known (quite incorrectly) as 'The Manor House', and then as 'The Old Parsonage', was claimed to be the honeymoon cottage on the authority of Mr. E. F. Blanchard, a contemporary of Dickens, who lived at Rosherville. The claims of 'Craddock's Cottage' were never accepted by the London Dickens Fellowship, and shortly after the Fitzgerald bust was erected a letter written by Dickens on his honeymoon from 'Mrs. Nash's' at Chalk was found. This cottage (No. 18 Lower Higham Road) was further west on the south side, next to the old *White Hart,* and was demolished in 1957.

Vicarage Lane is so called from the vicarage which was built in 1869 and stood on the east side. It was demolished about 1968 and a small estate built on the site. The previous vicarage was in Lower Higham Road, opposite the end of Vicarage Lane, and was later known as Great Clayne Farm. A re-fronted early 18th-century house, of the same style and period as 'West Court', it was demolished in 1963. As before noted the village road continues to loop into the main road which leads to the parish church of St. Mary.

Near the junction with the fields to the north was found the remains of a large Roman villa in 1961. A narrow roadway on the left leads to the Lower Road, and at the corner of this road stood until the Second World War *The Lisle Castle,* Chalk's third inn. This was destroyed by an aerial mine and remained in a derelict condition until totally demolished in 1956. In this lane were a row of cottages known as 'Links Cottages', from the fact that the second golf links was laid out there.

The church of St. Mary is largely of Early English date, with a late 12th-century north aisle. The dormer windows in this aisle are 19th-century work, the roof previously sweeping down to a low north wall. The 13th-century lancets in the chancel have been much restored. A later south aisle has been destroyed. The tower is a typical Kentish 15th-century one with projecting stair turret, and the porch with its quaint tippling figures which so intrigued Dickens, is of the same period. The porch cornice is Victorian; previously there was a pointed roof. The church suffered from a drastic Victorian restoration and underwent further considerable restoration in the early 1950s. It has a nave of three bays with north aisle, the western end of which is now a vestry for choir and priest. On the south side of the chancel is a 13th-century sedila and piscina with shelf. Inside the west door is a stoup.

On the east side of Church Lane is 'East Court', another of the Chalk manors. This part of the parish is still largely unbuilt on and was always quite separate from Chalk Street at 'West Court'.

Of its farms, that of Filborough is the oldest, being mentioned as early as 1220, when it was bought from John, son of Hugh de Nevill, by John, son of Henry de Cobham. It later passed into the hands of Henry VIII, who let it to James Reynolds of London, joiner, in 1545. A brass to a member of a family occupying Filborough, William Martyn and his wife Isabella, was placed in Chalk church after their death in 1416. They left money for 'Church Ales' and the porch figures may be connected with this. The house itself was an open hall with cross wing and inserted chimney and crown posts in both the main part and the wing and was restored by G. M. Arnold.

A member of the family of Lovelace, which was that of the poet of that name, designated himself as a 'gentleman of Chalke, where I was born'. His wish to give something to the poor of Chalk and his desire to be buried there do not seem to have been carried out.

Chalk is mentioned in Domesday, but this is not the earliest mention of the parish, there having been a 'witan' there shortly after 700 A.D. to confirm the Wilmington Charter of that year devised by Archbishop Berhtwald. It would appear that in 1390 Cobham College, then an abode of monks, owned land in the village, John Long being appointed vicar on the presentation of the Master and Brethren of the College. A John Pottkyn and his wife Constance are mentioned in records of wills, John's wife having formerly been the wife of Robert Martin, who died in 1456.

The area of Chalk before its incorporation into Gravesend was 1835 acres, its western boundary being for a considerable length that of the eastern boundary of Denton, but extending farther south to border Ifield before it turns east for about 1,200 yards to cross Thong Lane and leave the southern part of the lane in the parish of Shorne. To the east of Thong Lane the boundary line turns north for about 200 yards, then north-east irregularly for 1,000 yards to pass below the church at Deadman's Bottom (so called from the name of a local farmer) at about 250 yards on the eastern side, and so to the riverside 300 yards less or more of Shornemead fort.

In that part of the Chalk area more recently built over a Church of England church was built in 1965, dedicated to St. Aidan (architects, Northover and Northover of Tenterden). A parish hall was also built in 1965. Other places of religious congregation include a Community Centre and place of worship belonging to the Shaftesbury Society and a 'Full Gospel Church' in Valley Drive.

Chapter Twenty-One

THE PARISH OF IFIELD AND THE VILLAGE OF SINGLEWELL

WHILST IT IS POSSIBLE to convey to a reader a tolerably clear idea of the shape and place upon a larger map of the parishes of Denton and Chalk, the parish of Ifield offers no such easy depiction. The puzzling manner in which parts of the parish of Northfleet have intruded and separated one part from another have always been difficult to follow, and the inclusion of these within the Gravesend municipal boundary since 1935 has not lessened the difficulty. A map of Ifield before that date suggests a section of a patchwork quilt, with the eastern part of the parish running north and south across Watling Street, and divided from the western part north of Watling Street by a strip of Northfleet territory on the east side of Singlewell Road, which broadens out south of Watling Street, only retreating to the west sufficiently to allow Ifield church and rectory to preserve a place just inside the parish border.

Thus the ground upon which Harman Avenue, Orchard Avenue and Golf Links Avenue are built and the southern part of the golf links on the west side of Singlewell Road are in the old Ifield parish, whilst the land on the east side of that thoroughfare, including the recently-erected school, Westfield and Craggs farm are, or rather were, in the parish of Northfleet, as far as the eastern portion mentioned above.

Except for the church and rectory of Ifield, most of the parish was in common parlance Singlewell, a name arising from the old well (properly 'Shinglewell') which, with its winding gear, stood a few yards from the older Watling Street in the roadway which joins the recently-named Hever Road with Marlings Cross. During the First World

War the well was filled in and a granite slab placed there to record its earlier existence, and being inscribed appropriately. This slab was removed in 1952. (The widely-held opinion that the village was named 'Singlewell' because there was only one well in the parish was entirely erroneous, there being others in the district.) A legend of a miracle performed here by St. Thomas of Canterbury, whereby a panic-stricken girl, Salerna, was saved from drowning by the saint's intervention, may be taken as witness of the well's antiquity. The legend, translated from Latin MSS by the Rev. K. M. Ffinch, rector of Ifield, 1912–1938, is printed in *The History of Ifield and Singlewell* from Mr. Ffinch's notes.

Turning from the south end of Singlewell Road to the left we proceed along the older Watling Street of pre-1924 days, which is now known as Hever Court Road. The farm on the corner demolished in 1971, was known as Craggs Farm, and at one time the farmlands covered a considerable area to the north, extending nearly as far as Cross Lane. The houses on Hever Court estate were erected in 1957. Until these changes were wrought the thoroughfare was a narrow lane with a pond on the north side of the roadway overhung with elms. 'Hever Court', which gave its name to the road, was for many years the most imposing house in the village, itself standing upon the site of an earlier 'Hever Court', the original house of the Hever family, who removed to Hever, near Tonbridge, in 1331. The later 'Hever Court' was a 17th-century house of brick which bore over its dining-room window 'P.R.E. 1675'. During the Second World War it was occupied by the War Office as a barracks, and during that occupation a fire caused great damage to roof and walls: as a result it became derelict and was demolished in 1952. It had been formerly the property of Sir James Fergusson and Sir Thomas Colyer-Fergusson, his son.

On the eastern side of 'Hever Court' is a pathway leading to Gravesend across what was for many years arable land, and known as Singlewell Fields.

On the south side of the road unsuspected by many who have passed it by through the years is what remains of an old chapel which may date back to the period of the Salerna legend. The stucco front of the farmhouse, Chapel

Farm, gives no hint that the lower walls are some 2ft. 6ins. thick. The south wall, away from the road, is exposed and of flint and ragstone with a doorway and stone quoins of two windows which have been filled in. There are some written references to this chapel, and a fuller account is given in the *History* mentioned above.

A few yards farther east is the *George* inn which, during the 19th century, was a favourite house of refreshment of Gravesenders, who found it a convenient walking distance from home on summer evenings. An extension on the south in the 1930s opened its patronage to the coaches and lorries on the A2, and there is now a loopway to its successor, opened in 1971.

On the south side of the busy road a narrow thoroughfare of some antiquity leads to the tiny parish church of St. Margaret. While it has no great architectural pretensions, it is attractive in its rural setting. From its dimensions and the thickness of the walls it would seem that Ifield church is probably a small two-cell Norman fabric like Denton, Dode and Paddlesworth, but roughcast and interior plaster have concealed all the early features. There is, however, the remains of an inserted low side window on the south chancel wall, and a reference in an early 19th-century painting in the K. A. S. collection at Maidstone refers to lancets in the chancel. The present windows date from 1845, the cusping and tracery may have been copied from the 15th-century window at 'Ifield Court'. The previous church windows were also square headed. The rectory on the right-hand side of the lane was built in 1865 on the glebe land.

'Ifield Court', reached by a farm on the right, is a Georgian house built in 1745, standing on the site of a former manor house, a small fragment of which in ragstone with a three-light triple-cusped window, exists at the east end of the present house. Further medieval work was demolished in 1907, but, unfortunately, no illustration of this seems to have survived. In the reign of Elizabeth I it belonged to Sir John Garrard, Lord Mayor of London. There were formerly three manors of Ifield Court, Wells and Cossington, all in Northfleet parish. Earthworks in Cossington Wood probably mark the site of a deserted village or hamlet, and

Wells Field was to the south of the church. At the end of Church Lane, where the road branches for Nurstead, Sole Street and Cobham, was Toltingtrow Green, the meeting place of the Hundred of Toltingtrow, of which Northfleet, Ifield, Gravesend and Milton formed part (Denton and Chalk were in Shamel). The meeting place for the Hundred of Shamel seems to have been Gads Hill where there is a 'Court' Wood. In the 18th century the Hundred met at the *Duke of York* at Shorne.

PART FOUR

Chapter Twenty-Two

THE PARISH OF NORTHFLEET

IN THE LAST CHAPTER we dealt with a small part of the parish of Northfleet, which was intertwined with the parish of Ifield, and in this chapter the bounds of Northfleet parish will be dealt with, and its organisation. It immediately adjoins Gravesend to the west, but is of considerably greater area, about 3,000 acres, and extends far to the south. Its western boundary commences from a point in the River Thames in Northfleet Hope where a sweep to the north in the course of the river leaves a large tract of marsh, the eastern part of this marsh known as Botany Marsh is in Northfleet, the western part being in Swanscombe. The boundary runs across some saltings and then along a track known as Green Manor Way, and thence along the Lower Road to the main road which it crosses, and then to the railway, when it turns east to join Ebbsfleet, which it follows to Springhead, taking in the easternly part of the gardens once famous for its watercress. It then runs along Watling Street to a point about a quarter of a mile east of Springhead Road, whence it turns south and runs more or less parallel with the New Barn Road to a point near the reservoir of the Medway Water Board to the south of Fawkham Avenue. From here it turns east and runs to a point on the Wrotham Road just to the north of Nurstead Wood, where it crosses the road and runs between Nurstead Court and Nast Street and taking in Cossington Wood, runs to Church Lane, Ifield, just to the north of Toltingtrow Green. Then into the field opposite to include Wells Field before turning north to run with Cobham and Ifield, and thence to Singlewell village. It will be seen that in addition to Northfleet 'town' the parish includes such hamlets as Northfleet Green and Nash Street, the old built-up area of

Perry Street and the new estates at Shears Green, Istead Rise and Downs Road. The Northfleet Urban District Council which was merged with Gravesend on 1 April 1974 was set up under the Local Government Act of 1894, and its predecessor, the Northfleet Local Board of Health, was constituted at a meeting held on 9 July 1874.

We will now deal with the older part of Northfleet parish by following the main roads in a pattern similar to that adopted for Gravesend.

Chapter Twenty-Three

LONDON ROAD FROM THE GRAVESEND BOUNDARY TO THE 'LEATHER BOTTLE'

Together with the area between the main road, Granby Road and the River

IMMEDIATELY AFTER CROSSING the parish boundary the name of the road changes from Overcliffe to London Road. To the north lie Pier Road and Burch Road, which were laid out as part of a scheme for Rosherville New Town in 1830, by H. E. Kendal. A prospectus of the period states that 'this spot will ultimately become to Gravesend what St. Leonards is to Hastings and Broadstairs to Margate'. The houses with porches with Corinthian capitals at the south ends of these two roads and the Italianate houses in Lansdowne Square date from this period. At the foot of Burch Road on the west side stood the *Rosherville* hotel, also built by H. E. Kendal. This played its part in the Gravesend Yacht Week. It was used as a hospital during the First World War and then became flats and was demolished about 1968. At the foot of Burch Road was Rosherville pier, built in 1840, for the gardens traffic and for many years there was a ferry from this pier to Tilbury in the mornings and a return trip at night to cater for the 'commuters' who lived at Rosherville and travelled to London by the London, Tilbury and Southend railway.

At the south-west corner of Lansdowne Square was the entrance to Rosherville Gardens, laid out in 1837 by George Jones in a disused chalk pit lying between Crete Hall Road and London Road. They were a place of surpassing beauty and a favourite resort of Londoners. Adorned with small Greek temples and statuary set in the cliffs, there were terraces, an archery lawn, Bijou theatre, and Baronial Hall for refreshments, and at one time a lake. At night the gardens were illuminated with thousands of coloured lights and there were firework displays and dancing. Famous bands such as the American Sousa were engaged during the season. Blondin, the trapezist, performed on a tightrope stretched across a chasm in the cliffs. In 1857 as many as 20,000 visitors passed through the turnstiles in one week. By 1880 the gardens had reached the peak of their popularity and thereafter began to decline and in 1901 they were closed and came under the hammer. However, there was a brief revival in 1903 when they re-opened for the summer season only and so continued until 1911. They were then used as a location for some early films, and the archery lawn became a football ground. They were also occasionally opened for the local hospital fetes which had been held there since 1857. In 1926 part of the ground was sold to Henleys Cable Works, and they took over the remainder in 1937. There was, however, one last fete held in the remaining part of the gardens in 1936 before the area was cleared and the cliffs cut back for the new offices and factories of Henleys, now A.E.I.

On the other side of Crete Hall Road facing the river was Crete Hall, with its miniature park. Built by Benjamin Burch about 1800 it was later occupied by his son-in-law, Jeremiah Rosher. It was purchased by W. T. Henleys Telegraph Works, Ltd., in 1905, who built their Cable Works in the grounds, the first length of cable being produced in July 1906. Crete Hall became the residence of their local manager, the last to live there being Mr. T. Wright, and was later used as offices, being finally demolished in 1937. To the west was a house known as 'The Mount', and to the east Old Crete Hall stood on the site purchased by the Amalgamated Press in 1899. The road leading from London Road to Crete Hall Road, known as the Coach Road, was the private carriage drive to Crete Hall, and a Lodge at one time stood at the London Road end. The site now occupied by the South Eastern Electricity Generating Station was at one time known as Sheep's Head Hill, and the old *Red Lion* public house occupied a site nearer the river. It was here that Alfred Tolhurst built the Red Lion Cement Works about 1880. He was the first cement manufacturer to use locomotives to haul his chalk trucks.

In 1894 he built the Deepwater Wharf, a wooden T-shaped structure jutting 230 feet into the river, which for the first time enabled a large sailing vessel to be taken off a Thames wharf at dead low tide. The Red Lion works was closed during the First World War, together with the Imperial Cement Company's works adjoining. The site remained derelict between the wars, although the Deepwater Wharf continued to be used for mooring ships. In the 1939–1945 war the concrete anti-aircraft towers were built here and towed down to the mouth of the river for the protection of shipping. The site was finally cleared when the present generating station was built in 1951.

Proceeding along Crete Hall Road towards Northfleet the area between the road and the river was the site of Pitcher's dockyard. It was laid out by Thomas Pitcher in 1788 on ground levelled as a result of chalk workings. The first launch, that of *The Royal Charlotte* (123 tons) took place on 2 November 1789. In 1813 the Russian fleet was refitted in this yard. The yard was closed in 1825, but re-opened by William and Henry Pitcher, sons of the founder, in 1839, and became one of the largest yards on the river. For some years steamships were built here for the Royal Mail Packet Co., as well as for the government during the Crimean War. The yard finally closed in 1860. A scheme for much larger docks, including a dock large enough to take the *Great Eastern* was featured in the *Illustrated London News* in April 1859, but nothing came of it.

Pitcher built a castellated house and gate known as the 'Castle', using material from Old London Bridge, which was a feature of the waterside until about 1924. Adjoining was Dock Row, and a public house called *The Royal Charlotte*, after the first vessel launched from the yard. An annual fair and sports known as Royal Charlotte Fair were held here in the 1830s. The first Bowater's paper mill was built in 1926 on some 27 acres to the south of the road. It was on this site that there stood until 1955 a mass of chalk and clay (known as Caley Bank), some 80 feet in height, which had been left by the early chalk diggers. When the dockyard was in operation a flagstaff stood on the top and a small cannon which was fired when launches took place. In this area was the Northfleet brickfield which in the 1870s was worked by Messrs. Gay and Blackman. It later belonged to George Austin and had a small wharf at the foot of Granby Road. A curious brick building at the bottom of Granby Road demolished in 1954, known as the 'Mill House', was apparently erected as an engine house for a stationary engine used to haul trucks.

We have now covered the area between the Gravesend boundary and Granby Road, and we will now return to Pier Road to cover London Road between that point and Granby Road. Immediately opposite Pier Road is one of the entrances to Rosherville station (the other was opposite Burch Road where the South Eastern Electricity Board is now). This was opened in 1886 to cater for the garden traffic, and closed in 1933. The stationmaster's house still remains on the bank. The employment exchange was closed in 1973 when new offices were opened in The Grove. On the corner of Burch Road stood until 1964 St. Mark's vicarage, a charming ragstone Gothic conceit in the same style as the church. St. Mark's was built in 1855. The architects were Messrs. H. and E. Rose, and the cost and endowment were borne by the Rosher family. Mr. George Rosher was the patron, who also paid for the vicarage. The church was built of Kentish rag and Caen stone quoins and carvings. The rag weathered very badly, and extensive repairs were carried out in 1896 under W. and C. A. Bassett Smith, when the four stone angels which stood on supports round the spire were removed. The restoration of the spire was completed in 1901. A scheme to demolish Rosherville church has now been approved.

The land opposite the church now occupied by the bus depot (built in 1938), and the houses in Marina Drive and the adjoining roads was until about 1930 a small dairy farm known as Johnson's. On the north side of the road were large houses built in the 1830s as part of Rosherville new town and now demolished to make way for the more numerous modern ones. Fountain Court marks the site of the London Road entrance to Rosherville Gardens. This was opened in 1864 when a tower was built containing

21.—St. Mark's church, Rosherville, with vicarage, *c.* 1860

a clock with chimes on which tunes could be played. The clock was later removed and replaced by circular windows. The tower was demolished in 1938, but the entrance remained with its wall plaques until 1965 when the site was cleared. Remains of the Upper Walk and steps in the cliffs can be seen at the end of Fountain Walk, and the urns and statues now forming part of the ornamental gardens come from the old gardens.

Rural Vale was the first of the small roads to be laid out on the south side of London Road, the houses on the west side being built about 1845. At the end of Rural Vale was a brick-tower windmill, built in 1840 by Richard Young, which was 50 feet in height. It was acquired in 1858 by William Boorman, who with his sons were corn merchants in Milton Road, Gravesend, and was usually known as Boorman's mill. It ceased work in 1894 and was pulled down about 1916. The remaining roads in this area were laid out in the 1880s.

At the top of the next hill are Rosherville schools, built in 1871, as church schools by the Rosher family: it became in 1937 a junior mixed and infant school. It is built of flint with brick dressings as is the schoolhouse next door.

The houses between Rosherville schools and the *Leather Bottle* were built in the 1830s as part of the Calcraft-Ryder estate of 'Upper Northfleet'. 'De Warren House', about half-way along, was at one time the residence of Thomas Bevan the cement maker, and his initials figured in the iron railings. He was unseated as Liberal M.P. for Gravesend in 1881 because he gave his workers a day off with pay on election day to vote for him. These houses now in process of being acquired for demolition and re-development by the Northfleet Council and private developers.

Chapter Twenty-Four

THE HILL, SPRINGHEAD ROAD AND DOVER ROAD

LONDON ROAD JOINS Dover Road and Springhead Road (formerly Leather Bottle Lane) and then sweeps to the right to become The Hill. This area is the historic centre of Northfleet with the church forming the background. At the junction of Dover Road and Springhead Road stands the *Leather Bottle.* In the early 19th century it was still comparatively isolated, with stables at the rear (recently demolished to make way for the car park) and a sawpit and carpenter's yard in the field at the junction of Dover Road and London Road, where now is the library. Behind the *Leather Bottle* in Springhead Road was the old parish lock-up. Latterly used as a cottage it was demolished about 15 years ago. The land between Dover Road and Springhead Road was acquired by the government in 1806 (although troops seem to have camped here as early as 1763) and became known as Barrack Field. It was formerly called Harp Field. Here during the Napoleonic wars troops were quartered. A little further down Springhead Road at Snagg's Bottom on the west side is a timber-framed hall house of the late 15th or early 16th century, known as the 'Old Rectory'. It was probably the residence of the steward of the Rectorial Tithes which belonged to the Priory of Rochester. At the rear of the houses on the west side of Springhead Road in an area known as Church Field, occupied by a disused quarry, was the football ground, and it was here that the Saxon cemetery was found in 1899 when the ground was excavated: saucer brooches, a few weapons and cremation urns were found, which are in the local collection.

The Roman Catholic church was built in 1914 on the site of the horse tram depot as a memorial to Alfred Tolhurst, the solicitor and cement manufacturer. The architect was Sir Giles Scott, and the tower foreshadows that of his Liverpool cathedral. The builder was J. B. Lingham who lived at The Hill at the time. It is a fine example of 20th-century Gothic in brown brick. It is perhaps worthy of note that a mile further along the main road at Galley Hill is another modern Gothic church built for the cement maker Beazley White by Norman Shaw in 1894, and since 1972 also a Roman Catholic church. Just beyond the site of the Roman Catholic church was the Northfleet Tollgate. It was set up by the Turnpike Commissioners in 1860 as an additional gate to try to increase the tolls for the road which had been falling since the opening of the railway. The gate was financially successful, but only lasted until 1871, when the Trust was wound up. It occupied the site of the old village stocks and parish pound of which there are one or two drawings in existence. Opposite was the old *Queen's Head*, destroyed by fire in 1830. The oldest house now standing is No 31, formerly the *Plough* inn.

The area now used as a car park and between the wars as a site for the War Memorial, was the old village green, and at its north-west corner was a well. The buildings round this area are of various dates, the *Coach and Horses* and the betting shop adjoining, apparently being part of a timber-framed house. The Northfleet Manor House occupied a site to the north-east of the church, and was at one time used as a school kept by the curate. It was demolished in 1880.

The church dedicated to St. Botolph is one of the largest in Rochester Diocese and was a wealthy living, frequently held by an absentee incumbent. It dates from the early 14th century in the decorated Gothic (with the exception of two of the nave windows, which are perpendicular), and consists of a six-bay nave with north and south aisles and chancel. The tower was built in 1717 inside the old one which fell in the previous century. At the south-west corner is evidence of the original Saxon church, with long and short work on the quoins. Inside part of the arcade is 13th-century work. Perhaps the most interesting interior feature is the chancel screen which is early 14th century, the same period as the church. It retained its solid wooden doors until about 1830.

22.—Northfleet church, *c*. 1860

The chancel arch and the harsh sedilia in the chancel are both the work of E. W. Godwin in 1862, but there is an attractive piscina and sedilia in the south aisle, which are original, although the sub-deacon's seat was damaged in 1790 when W. H. Burch built a family pew here with 'a warming machine'. The altar dates from 1922 and the screen was erected in 1937 as a memorial to George Snelling and Charles Kean. The floors of both nave and chancel were raised during the Victorian restoration, and the well-known brass of Peter de Lacey (1375) lost its canopy and now has a small modern border. Northfleet at one time had at least 13 brasses, but of these only three remain, the other two being William Lye (1391) and William Rikhill and his wife Katherine (1433). All have been moved and mutilated (see *Archaeologia Cantiana,* Vol. XXXII, p. 36, for a full list of the lost brasses at Northfleet).

The chancel was refurnished and fitted up between 1862 and 1879, and the Victorian glass in the east window installed in 1861 as a memorial to the Prince Consort. The church schools were opened in 1838.

Chapter Twenty-Five

THE MAIN ROAD FROM GRANBY ROAD TO THE PARISH BOUNDARY WITH UNDERSHORE

ON LEAVING THE CHURCH and The Hill on the north side of the road just to the east of Granby Road was the forge, where horses were shod until the 1930s. On the opposite side of the road where there is now a small housing estate was the vicarage, built in 1834, on the site of an earlier one. It was demolished in 1961 when the present houses were built. The quarry to the west of the church was at one time a cherry orchard and a field here was called Vineyard Field, a reminder that the Archbishop of Canterbury had a vineyard at Northfleet in the 14th century. Most of the quarry on the north side of the road is now taken up by the new Northfleet Cement Works, opened in 1970. Here were formerly the Northfleet Engineering Works, owned by Alfred Horlock and the London Portland and Crown Cement Works. The site was at one time a shipbuilding yard owned by Mr. Calcraft, and here was built the first of the *Eagle* boats for the General Steam Navigation Company. In 1854 an ammunition works belonging to a German firm, Schliesinger and Wells, occupied the site and supplied cartridges for the Crimean War. An illustration of the works appears in the *Illustrated London News*.

On the waterside was 'Howard House', a red brick Queen Anne house, so named after Jeremiah Howard, a lime merchant, at the end of the 18th century, but built about 1717 for Francis Mackreth. Just to the east was Howard Square, a small square of late-18th-century houses occupied mostly by customs officers and watermen.

The *India Arms* at the foot of Lawn Road dates from the early 19th century, and adjoining it at one time there is said to have been a small fort with four guns manned by the Northfleet Volunteers, who at the time of the Nore

Mutiny manned the Gravesend blockhouse. At the top of Lawn Road was Lawn House or Northfleet Lodge. On the opposite side of the main road was Northfleet House (now the Council offices), built by M. Sturge, the cement manufacturer, and later occupied by Alfred Tolhurst. Its entrance gates were topped with whale harpoons. In the grounds the first council houses in Northfleet were built in 1926.

The main road from here now known as High Street was, at least from the 16th century, known as Bow Street, Stonebridge Hill being known as Fishermen's Hill. Opposite the schools was 'Bow House', sometimes known as 'Paddy Wadman's Folly'. The High Street schools were the first board schools in Northfleet and were built in 1884. The Factory Club (now the Blue Circle Club) was built by Mr. Bevan in 1878 for his cement workers (architects, Parr and Strong), and for many years contained a good organ which was used by The Northfleet Choral and other musical societies. Two former houses on the waterside should be mentioned, namely 'Hive House', on a site now covered by the old Bevan's works, and 'Orme House', on the waterside near the Creek, which tradition connects with Judge Jeffreys. It was apparently rebuilt in 1834 and demolished in 1872. A windmill at one time stood between Hive Lane and Lawn Road, and another pair of mills nearer Stonebridge Hill.

The appearance of Northfleet High Street has completely changed with the demolition of the shops and houses on the north side, and the development of The Hive as a shopping centre in the last few years. Beyond this lay Huggen's College, built in 1847 by John Huggens as almshouses, with its own chapel and croquet lawn. The architect was Mr. W. Chadwick. It was demolished in 1968 and new bungalows and a new chapel built on part of the site, and the remainder sold to the Council, who have built blocks of hideous flats, now known as Wallis Park. The chaplain's house which is all that survives of the former college was originally a farmhouse.

At the foot of Stonebridge Hill was Plough Pond, fed by the Ebbsfleet, and controlled by a sluice. The 'stone' bridge over the Ebbsfleet was built in 1634 to replace an earlier one and was itself replaced by a brick one on a more

23.—Huggen's College entrance gates, *c.* 1860

convenient line about 1790. At this point the first turnpike road, which ran from Northfleet to Strood, commenced (see Chapter Twenty). It was also near here that the watermill, possibly a tide-mill, mentioned in Domesday Book, was probably situated. Hasted mentions that it was still in existence at the end of the 18th century, when it was used for stucco. To the north Grove Road runs down to the waterside, passing the site of Grove House, at one time the residence of Mr. Butchard, the owner of the Tower Cement Works, one of a number of small works situate round the Creek. The best known of these was Robbins, as it was here that Aspdin, one of the inventors of Portland cement built his first bottle kilns. The original kiln, which was damaged in the last war, has been restored and preserved by the A.P.C.M. Robbins was taken over by Thomas Bevan in 1853, who with his partners, Mr. Knight, a chemist from Rochester, and Mr. Sturge, re-opened the works, and with their Pyramid Brand soon became one of the leading cement manufacturers. They built their own barges at Northfleet and also had a cooperage and staveyard, where barrels for the cement were made. Mr. Bevan's sons, Robert, Wilfred and Edmund, followed him, but sold out to the A.P.C.M. in 1900. In 1905 small rotary kilns were introduced, and in 1926 the works were rebuilt with four rotary kilns, then the largest in Europe. At the same time a new deep water jetty was built.

Between Bevan's works and the *India Arms* were the Northfleet gasworks.

Before leaving this part of Northfleet mention should be made of the Roman villa site near the Ebbsfleet, excavated by Mr. W. H. Steadman between 1909 and 1911, which revealed also a small lime kiln, evidence of the long use of chalk for this purpose in this area, and also of Baker's Hole with its early flint workshop, which produced some of the best-known examples of the Levallois industry in Britain. They are now in the British Museum and there are some flint implements in the local museum from Baker's Hole.

Chapter Twenty-Six

PERRY STREET AND SOUTH NORTHFLEET

SPACE DOES NOT PERMIT of a perambulation of the rest of Northfleet, but one or two places of historical note will be mentioned in this last chapter. *Perry Street*—the name appears as early as 1281—was one of the old hamlets. Murrels farm in Vale Road is a much-altered timber-frame building (there is a date 1687 on it); opposite is 'Kingston House' of the early 18th century. The *Six Bells* in Coldharbour Road had a forge adjoining, and there were a number of old cottages in Coldharbour Road between here and Scrattons farm which made up 'Old' Perry Street. Shears Green appears in 1357, and Durndale was a one-time manor. The roads to the south of Perry Street date from the 1830s, as does the Northfleet or west side of Victoria Road. All Saints' church was built in 1871, the architect being James Brooks. At the end of Fiveash Road was a smock-mill built by John Fiveash in 1795, who at one time worked the mill on Windmill Hill. It later belonged to a Mr. Snowden, and was pulled down towards the end of the 19th century. On the opposite side of the road is a building now used as a factory which was originally the tramway depot with an entrance from Dover Road. The first horse tramway was opened in 1883 between The Hill, Northfleet, and St. James church, Gravesend, later extended to Trinity church. The depot and stables then occupied the site of the Roman Catholic church on The Hill. A short experimental electric line (the first in the south of England) was opened between The Hill and Northfleet station in 1889, but this ceased operating about a year later. The system was finally electrified in 1902 and extended to Swanscombe and with a loop via Dover Road and Pelham Road, and a branch up Windmill Street to *The Old Prince of Orange*. It closed in February 1929, the first system in the London area to be abandoned. Some six of the original open-top trams were fitted closed tops by Beadle Bros. of Dartford in 1923, and were the first public service vehicles in the district to have any protection from the weather on the top deck. The first closed-top buses were Leylands, which replaced the trams in February 1929.

In concluding perhaps mention should be made of Wombwell Hall. Now part of the Technical School, the present building, erected in 1860 for Thomas Colyer, occupies the site of at least two earlier houses of this name. The first erected in 1471 by Thomas Wombwell, who came from a village of that name in Yorkshire, and the second by James Fortrey in 1663. The last family to live there were the Colyer-Fergussons, who were there until 1937. Evidences of deneholes and tunnels have been found in this area.

24.—Aspdin's Cement Kilns and Joseph Aspdin, *c.* 1825 (courtesy of A.P.C.M. Ltd.)

Chapter Twenty-Seven

BIBLIOGRAPHY

THERE ARE *Histories of Gravesend* by Robert Pocock (1797), Robert Pierce Cruden (1843), F. A. Mansfield (1922), and Alex J. Philip (1954) (which incorporates an earlier volume of his of 1914). In addition George Mathews Arnold published a life of Robert Pocock, Gravesend's first historian in 1883, a lecture on 'Gravesend in the Very Time of Old' (1896), and on Denton in 1901. W. H. Hart published extracts from Public Records relating to Gravesend and District in 1878. There is a *History of Northfleet,* by Rev. S. H. Cooke (1942), *Ifield and Singlewell,* by Rev. K. M. Finch (revised and edited by R. H. Hiscock, 1957), *The Parish Churches of Gravesend and the Burial Place of Princess Pocahontas,* by R. H. Hiscock (1957), *The Story of Milton Parish,* by J. Benson and R. H. Hiscock (1955), *Field Names of Gravesend,* by E. R. Green, and *A Historical Sketch of Gravesend Fort and Milton Chantry,* by V. T. C. Smith (1965).

There are a long series of Guide Books, starting in 1817. The *Pictorial Guide* (1844), *Miss E. Brabazon's Month at Gravesend* (1863), J. R. S. Clifford (1886), and the various editions of *The Homeland Handbook* from 1906 are probably the best. All these books and numerous other guides and local directories from the mid-19th century are in the public library, which also has an extensive collection of drawings, prints, maps, photographs, postcards and other local material. The various *County Histories,* such as Lambarde, Kilburn, Harris, Hasted, Leland, Jessup, and the *Victoria County History* all contain references to the town. *The Buildings of England West Kent and the Weald,* by John Newman (1969) contains references to the existing buildings in the town. The volumes of *Archaeologia Cantiana,* from 1858 also contain local material. The *Transactions of the*

Gravesend Historical Society since 1954 contain much of local interest.

The main manuscript sources are the archives of the Gravesend Corporation, and the material housed at the library and at the Kent Archives Office at Maidstone. The great debt owed by all researchers in this field to those who have gone before cannot be over-estimated, and Mr. Benson was always conscious of this in his articles which appeared over the years in *The Gravesend and Dartford Reporter*, the volumes of which are themselves a rich source of local events for over 100 years, as are those of the other local papers, such as *The Gravesend Standard* and the old Gravesend edition of the *Kent Messenger*.

APPENDIX

THE GRAVESEND PIERS

WITH THE DEVELOPMENT of Gravesend as a watering place and the coming of the pleasure steamer traffic to the town, the first half of the 19th century saw the development of piers on the river bank.

At the beginning of the century the principal landing place was the ancient Town Quay at the bottom of High Street, which had long been one of the possessions of the Gravesend Corporation, and from which it derived a certain amount of income from landing fees.

In 1827 the Corporation took steps to rebuild the quay and improve its approaches. The inn known as *The Christopher* which narrowed the entrance to the quay was purchased and pulled down, and after public meetings to gain support, an Act of Parliament was obtained giving the Corporation power to build a new quay and to raise £7,000 on bonds secured upon a 1d. toll on all landing or departing from the new quay. A new stone-built quay with improved facilities was then built, with the small square and *Pier* hotel occupying the remainder of the old *Christopher* site. The quay was opened in 1829. Passengers from the steamers to the quay were rowed to the quay in watermen's wherries at a fee of 4d. per head, which was popular with the watermen, though not with the passengers or the steamer companies. A year later in 1840 Mr. Pitcher, who had a shipyard at Northfleet, opened a temporary pier at Northfleet, which was so successful that Gravesend people began to fear loss of traffic, and a project for the construction of a Gravesend pier was begun. A Bill was presented to parliament for power to build a pier on the site of the quay. This was resisted by the watermen, and finally rejected by the House of Lords. The Corporation then resolved to erect a temporary pier and to promote yet another Bill before parliament. The temporary pier was erected in 1832, and just before its completion was smashed up in a watermen's riot, to be rebuilt by the Corporation at considerable expense. The second Bill before parliament was successful after a compromised arrangement with the watermen, which was to prove expensive, and the Corporation authorised to build a pier and raise £12,000 to meet the expense, again on bonds secured on tolls. The pier was built and opened in 1834, but very considerable extravagance on the part of the Corporation incurred large debts in addition to the £12,000 bonds.

In 1835 Blockhouse Fort came on the market and was acquired by some councillors on their own account, who immediately erected a temporary pier called the Terrace Pier, in competiton with the Town Pier. This was followed by the Municipal Reform Act 1835, under which the old Corporation was ejected and a more or less new body of councillors elected. The new council immediately began litigation with the Terrace Pier party, which was inconclusive, expensive, and went on until 1842, when both parties were financially exhausted.

During this time a permanent pier was erected at Rosherville in Northfleet, and another pier with a relatively short life at Marine Parade, to the western end of the town.

In 1842 a contract was entered into between the Corporation and the Terrace Pier party for the Terrace Pier and gardens to be sold to the Corporation for £42,500, the sale to be completed as soon as the Terrace Pier Co. had constructed a new and permanent pier. The Royal Terrace Pier was then erected, but through a series of complicated evasions the contract to sell to the Corporation was never completed.

At this stage free competition between the two piers forced landing tolls down to unprofitable levels, and neither party was in a position to compete with the railway from London to Gravesend, which was finally opened in 1849. By 1852 Gravesend Corporation was bankrupt, and the bondholders had appointed a receiver of the Town Pier, who was quite unable to make the pier earn enough even to pay the interest, whilst the unsecured creditors levied execution on the Corporation's furniture at the pier and town hall, including its regalia and even the mace, aldermen's robes, and the jury box, and the mortgagees of the other assets of the Corporation, such as the town hall, put a bailiff into walking possession to protect their security against the other creditors. The Royal Terrace Pier continued for a time to cater for the fading tripper traffic from London, in the teeth of growing competition from Rosherville Pier and Rosherville Gardens.

For many years the Corporation rented back its furniture and regalia from its creditors by a complicated hire purchase arrangement until the old debts were at last liquidated. The council remained yearly tenants of the town hall until 1881 in which year Mr. G. E. Sharland, the town clerk, reorganised the town's finances and bought back the freehold in the town hall for £6,250, and redeemed the regalia and movables for £311. On 12 February that year he announced 'satisfaction of all judgments against the Corporation'.

Finally the Town Pier was sold by the receivers with parliamentary consent to the Tilbury and Southend railway in 1884 for £8,600, and in 1895 the Royal Terrace Pier Company went into liquidation, the Terrace Gardens were sold to a speculative builder, and the pier to a new company belonging to the local pilots.

INDEX

N.B. Some roads and streets mentioned in the text are not indexed but can be found in the appropriate chapter.

CORRECTIONS AND ADDITIONS

Page 6	The architect of the Baptist Church was John Gould Junior; the builder was his father.
Page 11	The colonnade market was built in 1818, architect Charles Fowler who was the architect of Covent Garden and Hungerford markets.
Page 16	In 1643 Lady Deborah Moody (nee Dunch) sailed from Gravesend to found Gravesend (now part of Brooklyn), New York. Line 6 of the second para. should read '1873' not '1783'.
Page 53	The *Clarendon* was opened as a hotel in 1842 when the building was purchased by John Chaplin of Rochester.
Page 55	The Literary Institute was built in 1842, architects Messrs. Cobham and Wright. It cost £3,000.
Page 59	The architects of the 1906 Methodist Church were Messrs. Morley & Sons of Bradford, the builders were A. E. Tong. Derek Buckler & Partners carried out a later restoration.
Page 61	Park House, built in 1835, became Queens College in 1842.
Page 65	An excavation by the Gravesend Historical Society in 1976 established that Milton Church never had an actual chancel.
Page 84	Gravesend Rifle Club had its H.Q. and range at the *White Post* which was used by the Home Guard during the 1939-45 war.
Page 86	The station portico is Tuscan. It has now (1978) been restored and a new balustrade has been provided by British Rail.
Page 91	Mention should have been made of Huggins Bungalows at the junction of Cross Lane and Wrotham Road. Generally known as Tipperary Cottages, they were built just after the first war, the land given by Sir Thomas Colyer-Fergusson in memory of his son, Captain T. R. Colyer-Fergusson, V.C. The money was raised by Mrs. Huggins, wife of Ald. H. Huggins, and opened on 29 April 1922 by Lord Desborough.
Page 101	The architect of Milton Mount College was C. E. Robins of Southampton. Its first Headmistress was Miss Selina Hadland, a pioneer in women's education, and was the first school to teach domestic science. In 1915 it moved to the Royal Agricultural College at Cirencester and in 1920 to Crawley.
Page 103	At No. 1, Portland Villas, and later at 94, Windmill Street, lived Richard Austin Freeman the novelist and creator of 'Dr. Thorndyke', the detective.

Page 112 The first houses in Warwick Terrace were built on Gutteridges Playing Fields in 1898.

Page 113 In 1924 Sir Alan Cobham ran air trips from a field to the south of King's Drive for five shillings, and in 1931 a Roman Burial Site was found in the garden of No. 27, King's Drive.

Page 114 The Sun Pound (for impounding straying animals) was at the junction of Old Road East and Cross Lane, to the west of the present Post Office. The horse trough was erected in the centre of the square in 1903 in memory of Frederick and Annie Martina Gibbon.

Page 121 The last blacksmith was A. Mann, who retired in 1953.

Page 125 The 'new' Watling Street was opened by the Prince of Wales (later Duke of Windsor) in 1924.

Page 144 'Roman' cement was manufactured by James Parker at Northfleet from about 1795 and 'Terrace' cement from 1818. Ashdin's Northfleet works were opened in 1848; his patent registered in 1825.